MW01492949

PFC. William Harvey Calhoon

September 12, 1922 – December 19, 2000

A Son's Letters to his Father

At the Front
1942–1945

TEC 5 US ARMY WORLD WAR II

One of 12 million regular guys
– One special son

ISBN 978-0-9977956-4-6

Published in the United States by Yesteryear Publishing.

Copyright 2016 by Yesteryear Publishing.

Yesteryear Publishing

P.O. Box 311

Hummelstown, PA 17036

www.yesteryearpublishing.com

yesteryearpublishing@gmail.com

(717) 566-3907

Based on letters written by a young soldier during World War II, *A Son's Letters to his Father* is compelling reading. Bill Calhoon, Class of 1941 who could have grown up in your hometown, was described by an early reviewer of the book as a regular GI, a simple man who understood the complexity of the war in which he found himself, not having any idea that he would not see his wife or as-yet-unborn child until the little boy was three years old. Bill was faithful in writing to both his wife and his father despite the fact that soldiers' letters were censored as to war campaigns and locations. However, because the letters are masterfully narrated in the context of the history, today's reader, with even a limited knowledge of WWII, is immersed in the daily coping on the homefront and the events in the Philippines as they were happening.

Authored by **Judith T. Witmer, Ed.D.**, Principal, Yesteryear Publishing

Designed by **E. Nan Edmunds**, Yesteryear Publishing

A Guide to the Reader

Parents, Siblings, Wife, Child, Nephew and Niece of William H. Calhoon

—who lived during the time, appeared in, or are noted in this book

Parents:

John D. Calhoon, Father, addressed as "Pappy" or "Daddy"
Mary Bear Calhoon, Mother, who died when Bill was twelve years old

Siblings:

George, oldest brother
Clarence, brother, known as "Clam" or "Clem"
John D., brother, known as "Skip"
Francis, brother, known as "Pud"
Edgar, brother, known as "Eggie" or "Eggy"
Mary, sister, known as "Sis"
Helen, sister

Wife:

Geraldine Romaine (Heisey) Calhoon, known as "Jerry"

Child:

William Harvey Calhoon, Jr.

Nephew:

Larry, son of Mary; Mary and Larry lived with Pappy
    during the War.

Niece:

Barbara Ann, daughter of Helen

Table of Contents

Table of Contents

Beginnings
World War II: 1941–June 1943

William Harvey Calhoon, born September 12, 1922 in Middletown, Dauphin County, Pennsylvania, was one of eight children, reared by their widowed father, John D. Calhoon, following the untimely death of William's mother, Mary Bear Calhoon in 1934. John Calhoon, who had grown up in a household with a step-mother, vowed that the same fate would never befall his own children. The Calhoons were a devout family with solid values, devoted to each other, and active in their church. William H. Calhoon was the fifth of six sons in this family and was twelve years old when his mother died.

The summer before he turned seventeen and would be entering his junior year in high school, William (Bill) Calhoon had attended a camp sponsored by the Sons of Veterans Reserves in Bethlehem, Pennsylvania and, while there, had sent postcards to two of his brothers, Edgar and John, thus early establishing a habit of corresponding with his family.

The roots of the Sons of Veterans Reserves (SVR) date back to 1881 with the "Cadet Corps" of the Grand Army of the Republic (GAR)—the largest Union Veterans organization and which had formed in 1866 after the Civil War. In 1881, following the Civil War, the members of the GAR encouraged the formation of their sons as the Sons of Union Veterans of the Civil War (SUVCW). These units eventually became known as the Sons of Veterans Reserve, when the Sons of Union Veterans of the Civil War moved toward a more patriotic and educational organization in design.

Many local organizations of the Sons of Union Veterans Camps formed reserve military units which volunteered their services during the Spanish-American War, World War I, and with the National Guard. Just prior to World War I, over 5,000 men wore the blue uniform of the SVR and, as late as the 1930's, several states regarded their local SVR units as a military training component.

Joseph Bear (who was William's grandfather), born in Cumberland County on September 18, 1834 married Mary E. Shetron; he died on April 21, 1901. He was a private in Company D, 202nd Regiment of the Pennsylvania Volunteers in the Civil War as a member of the Union Army (dates of service: 9/2/1864 – 8/3/1865).[1]

Among the children of Joseph and Mary Shetron Bear was a daughter named Mary Bear who married John D. Calhoon. The son of Mary Bear and John D. Calhoon was **William Harvey Calhoon.** This lineage assured Bill, as well as his brother Edgar two years later, a place in the Sons of Veterans Reserves (SVR). Importantly, there was support in this household for Bill to attend such military training—at least in the summer of 1939.

June 21, 1939

Sent to his brother Edgar was this postcard showing a Retirement Home for the Widows of Moravian Ministers:

"I am having a swell time; didn't have over 2 hrs. sleep since I got here."

June 21, 1939

Bill sent this postcard picturing the ramp of the Hill-to-Hill Bridge to his brother John D:

"Sorry that I didn't write before. But I was so busy that I couldn't. I was on guard duty 2 days."

In the Middletown High School 1941 Yearbook, *The Blue and Gold*, William Calhoon's classmates described him as being "the 'still life' of the party and not the noisy sort." While viewed as quiet, he was an active member of the Booster Club as a freshman, sophomore, and senior; a member of the Red Cross Club his sophomore year; held a position on the Raiders Football team as a sophomore; and ran track his freshman and sophomore years. His nick-name was "Buck" which he earned from his friends and family because, as family lore tells, he sometimes rode a buckboard to school. Well-rounded and well-respected, Bill could have had absolutely no idea of what was in store for him as a member of what would be known by history as "The Greatest Generation."

In the spring of 1941 William was graduated from Middletown High School, hearing in the distance the drums of war in Europe. But Europe was an ocean away and, like many young men in the area of Hershey, Pennsylvania in the early 1940s, he sought employment after graduation in the Hershey Chocolate factory, a job with security in a nation not yet totally out of the Great Depression. In 1941 the factory was hiring a number of new workers to replace those who were enlisting in the service, and Bill was hired immediately as a "candy packer conveyor."

Shortly after being hired, Bill rented a room at the Hershey Community Building (built in 1933 and owned by Hershey interests), as did many other single men in the area. He had only to cross the street to enter the factory where he worked. There was a trolley between Hummelstown and Hershey which Bill used to visit his sweetheart, Jerry Heisey, who lived with her parents in Hummelstown.

No doubt Bill and Jerry spent some time enjoying Hershey Park in the days when the park was for the townspeople and there was no charge for admission; there also was free entertainment and an annual community picnic held by the citizens of Hummelstown with most of the town in attendance and many going to the park on the trolley which had a "spur" to the park.

Bill, like many men at this time, likely because of the rumblings of war, joined the Pennsylvania Reserve Defense Corps which described him as nineteen years of age with brown hair, a medium complexion, and five feet, seven inches in height. There he was to serve until he was officially discharged from the Reserves on November 15, 1942 at which time he was inducted into the Army of the United States. In so doing he would be one of the 3,030,407 men[2] who enlisted in 1942, joining a number of his own classmates of 1941, other young men who had been graduated in the spring of 1942, as well as the many more who left their senior class of 1943 to enlist and to defend their country.

Bill had first met the girl he would marry at their country church (Geyers Methodist Church on Geyers Church Road in Middletown) when they were youngsters. Initially he had thought this young girl had been sent from the city and referred to her as the "Fresh Air Kid," a term used for city children who were hosted by farm families so that the city children could enjoy the "fresh air" of the country.

It didn't take too many years for William to learn that Geraldine ("Jerry") Heisey was from a small town nearby and they likely would have teased each other about their rival high schools, as Jerry attended Hummelstown High School from which she was graduated in 1941 whereas Bill, as noted above, was a graduate of nearby Middletown High School. The summer following their graduation, on July 18, 1942, Bill and Jerry were married at this same church and took a "wedding trip" (as it was termed) to Gettysburg, then a popular honeymoon destination. As Jerry was the only surviving child from a family of three girls, she welcomed becoming part of the much larger Calhoon family.

The future looked promising for the young couple, even though their lives, along with the lives of everyone else in the United States, had changed that quiet Sunday afternoon, December 7, 1941, on the Eastern seaboard when news of Pearl Harbor began to leak. At first there was nothing definite, just something about a problem somewhere in or near Pearl Harbor. By evening families were gathered around their radios waiting for any news, but anticipating the worst. They sat silently through the programs of "Jack Benny," "Edgar Bergen and Charlie McCarthy," and "One Man's Family," waiting to hear what their president would say on his regular Sunday evening "Fireside Chat" about this most unusual and frightening event.

What not everyone was aware of, however, is that earlier in the year, following increased tension between Japan and several other powers, including the United States, Britain and the Netherlands, many countries in South East Asia and the Pacific began to prepare for the possibility of war. By December 1941, the combined defense forces in the Philippines were organized into the US Army Forces in the Far East (USAFFE), which eventually included the Philippine Army's 1st Regular Division, 2nd Division, and 10 mobilized reserve divisions, along with the United States Army's Philippine Department.

General Douglas MacArthur had been recalled from retirement by the U.S. War Department and named commander of USAFFE on July 26, 1941. MacArthur had been the Military Advisor to the Philippine Commonwealth and had accepted control of the Philippine Army, tasked by the government of the Philippines with reforming an army made up primarily of reservists lacking equipment, training, and organization.

On July 31, 1941 MacArthur took command and organized USAFFE into four tactical commands with the Philippine 71st Infantry Division serving as a reserve. As of November 30 the strength of the US Army Troops in the Philippines, including Philippine units, was 31,095. Around 3:00 a.m. local time on December 8, 1941 news reached the Philippines that an attack on Pearl Harbor was in progress.

The Far East Air Force lost fully half of its planes when the Philippines was attacked by air and over the next few days the island was all but destroyed. The conclusion was that this first day after the attack on Pearl Harbor, was "a disorganized business" for which no commanders were "really at fault" because no one was "geared for war."

Among the civilian citizens in the United States, very little—if any—of this action in the Philippines was known, hearing only that something foreboding had happened and that nearly everyone was gathered around a radio waiting to hear from their president.

However, that evening of December 7 (Western Hemisphere), because he was in private session with his military advisers, President Roosevelt was unavailable to speak to the nation. His wife, Mrs. Eleanor Roosevelt, replaced him, addressing the country from the viewpoint of a mother who had three sons in the war zone—one in military service on a destroyer and two living in coastal cities in the Pacific. "I feel as though I were standing upon a rock and that rock is my faith in my fellow citizens," she stated with confidence.[3]

No listener that evening criticized Mrs. Roosevelt's high-pitched voice, for everyone felt a commonalty with the President's family, all of them dealing with thoughts of their own sons, husbands, and brothers, and perhaps even themselves in danger should the United States go to war.

The following day at noon, 60 million Americans were at their radios to hear Franklin D. Roosevelt speak briefly and simply to his Cabinet, both houses of Congress, and the Supreme Court,

> "Yesterday, December 7, 1941—a date which will live in infamy—the United States of America was suddenly and deliberately attacked by naval and air forces of the Empire of Japan."

The president's speech concluded with these words, "I ask that the Congress declare that since the unprovoked and dastardly attack by Japan on Sunday, December 7, 1941, a state of war has existed between the United States and the Japanese Empire."[4] The resolution passed with only one dissenting vote. The United States was at war with Japan. The following day, December 8, Germany and Italy declared war on the United States and the United States immediately reciprocated.

Young men rushed to volunteer for military service and newspaper reporters were there to cover the event, whether the enlistees were Joe down the street or Pennsylvanian James Stewart, who had won the 1940 Oscar for *The Philadelphia Story*.

Actually, the preparation for the almost inevitable coming war had already begun in earnest for the United States years earlier on November 14, 1938 when a White House conference (following the Munich crisis of September) became the springboard for Army mobilization as well as for new war planning. By November 30, the War Plans Division had produced a new blueprint for an unpretentious, balanced Army expansion, over a 2-year period, with from 167,000 to 280,000 Regular Army enlisted, and from about 190,000 to 240,000 National Guard enlisted.

In 1939 the Basic Mobilization Plans were followed quickly by the Protective Mobilization Plan, 1939 revision, for expanding and equipping the Army, and the Industrial Mobilization Plan, 1939 revision, for the economic mobilization of the nation. Specifically, following the outbreak of war in Europe on September 1, 1939, President Roosevelt on September 8 proclaimed a state of national emergency, the basis for much emergency action, until the event of December 1941 confirmed the wisdom of having made these preparations.

That September 1939 proclamation provided for a two-stage expansion to increase Regular and Reserve Army strength of July 1, 1939 to become Regular Active, 189,867 (174,000 enlisted) (50,000 overseas) (210,000 expiated authorized); National Guard 200,000; Reserves, 110,000.

In September 1940 the Burke-Wadsworth Act was passed by Congress and Selective Service (which would be known as "the draft") was born. In October registration of men between the ages of 21 and 36 began. Then in November 1942 the draft age expanded to men 18 to 37 years of age.

At the Front 1942–1945

With the specter of this draft hanging over the heads of all young, able-bodied men in this age group, most were faced with a decision of (1) taking their chances when "their number came up" or (2) enlisting. Most who were of draft age and already members of the individual states' Reserve Defense Corps enlisted into one of the branches of the military service.

There is evidence that William H. Calhoon may actually have enlisted on May 1, 1942 at Harrisburg. The Enlistment Record notes that he was "serving in (the) **first** enlistment period at date of discharge." More enlightening is the information on this document that he had had prior service in the "Sons of Veterans Reserve, entering in February 1937 and that he had served four years as a Private, one year as a Private First Class in June 1939 and then was made Acting 1st Sergeant in September 1941, holding that rank until his induction into the Army of the United States on the 15th day of November, 1942." (Signed, Richard M. Johnston, Captain, Company E, 2nd Regiment.)

The United States found itself faced with a mammoth charge in December 1941. Ill-equipped and wounded, the nation was at war with three formidable adversaries. It had to prepare to fight on two distant and very different fronts, Europe and the Pacific. America needed to quickly raise, train, and outfit a vast military force. At the same time, it had to find a way to provide material aid to its hard-pressed allies in Great Britain and the Soviet Union.

Meeting these challenges would require massive government spending, conversion of existing industries to wartime production, construction of huge new factories, changes in consumption, and restrictions on many aspects of American life. Government, industry, and labor would need to cooperate. Contributions from all Americans, young and old, men and women, would be necessary to build up what President Roosevelt called the "Arsenal of Democracy."

In the months after Pearl Harbor, the nation swiftly mobilized its human and material resources for war. The opportunities and sacrifices of wartime would change America in profound, and sometimes unexpected, ways.

Senior classes in high schools began watching their classmates leave school before graduating in order to enlist. Evacuation drills began in most schools and senior class plays were modified to re-cast male roles.

Those of high school age saw their classmates heading to war instead of college, and to some of those young men, the excitement and aura of "serving one's country" overrode the fear that they might not return. Many tried to hold onto their ties to their classmates as evidenced by an excerpt from letters sent by those in the service to their classmates, "...when is Class Night and the rest of the social events that go with graduation? I'll sure be thinking of you kids the night they give out diplomas."[5]

Yet, for some reason, the 1942 yearbook in Hummelstown barely mentioned the war except to dedicate *The Tatler* to a teacher, "May his volunteer service to his country bring him many rich rewards." Later in the book is the mention of dedicating "this page ... to the thousands of boys...especially the local lads who are fighting for their lives and ours." The book also mentions by name and with a photo of the only casualty from the high school to that point. The class history says nothing about the war situation except its final words, "we ... sail into the somewhat clouded future."[6]

Very likely Bill Calhoon, similar to many others of his age, felt a calling to serve his country and to become part of a movement to protect liberty. Perhaps he also saw an opportunity to "better himself" as he later indicated in a letter to his father, mentioning the opportunities in military specialty programs to be trained for a later civilian job.

Indeed, the military did offer opportunities far beyond serving in what was beginning to look like a major worldwide war. Bill was inducted on November 5, 1942, with his Date of Entry into Active Service noted as November 19, 1942, with both oaths taken in Harrisburg, the state capital.

Thus, William Harvey Calhoon became one of well over 16 million men and women, over 12 percent of the total United States population at the time, who would be enrolled in the armed forces during what would quickly be known as World War II.

After enlisting, Bill was sent to one of what would be widely known as <u>Reception Centers,</u> installations for the processing of newly procured manpower, including completion of all necessary records, issue of individual equipment, classification as to occupation, completion of immunization for smallpox and typhoid, assignment, and forwarding to tactical units or to other installations, called Replacement Centers. The stay of inducted men at Reception Centers was approximately two weeks.

An important function of the Reception Centers was a personal interview of each man. A qualification card then was prepared for each and based upon this information, verified in some instances by testing, inducted men would be placed where they could do the job they would know how to do best and where the Army could gain the most from their service. The men would then be forwarded either directly to the tactical units or other installations, or to <u>Replacement Centers.</u>

At these Replacement Centers, enlisted men received what was termed their basic military training and they were converted, in fact, from civilians to soldiers. Here their Classification Cards were rechecked, and they were given aptitude and other psychological tests as might have been required. Upon completion of the training course, they were ready for assignment to a particular unit.

World War II on the Home Front

Historians agree that there was something very special about this "Greatest Generation," and despite all of the destruction to lives and property that wars bring, the Second World War is unique in the history of the United States in that it captured the spirit of an entire country in an effort more united than at any other time. Many agree that it was likely the economic hardships of the Great Depression that steeled the country's resolve to get through the adversities of war.

While perhaps that spirit of determination by the entire country has been identified more clearly in retrospect, persons of any age who lived during that wartime have said that "people banded together" and the whole thrust of living focused on "the war effort," from factories retooling to women joining the Armed Forces, and from the children's contributions by collecting reusable items to composers creating the music of wartime. It was a very intense time, but one recalled as the citizenry's being instilled with a deep sense of service to others.

Because America was a major industrial power, the machinery was already in place for converting production from domestic needs to the tools for war—tanks, jeeps, ships of all sizes, submarines, small-bore rifles, and large artillery pieces. One of the foremost examples of what could be done when necessary is the Henry Kaiser plant which built the Liberty transport ships, using prefabricated sections, in under seven days. (According to legend, this completed-in-less-than-a-week ship allowed for Mr. Kaiser to win a bet with a competitor that he could do just that.)

To support the war effort, six and a half million women went to work in factories, 350,000 joined the Armed Forces, and countless others assumed leadership roles in the community.

Children went on a modern crusade, gathering everything from scrap metal to newspapers and silkweed; buying defense stamps once a week at school; and donating toiletry items, packing them in Junior Red Cross boxes to send overseas. All of these efforts were planned—and succeeded—as morale boosters on the home front.

Everyone, young and old, realized that the way of life they had known was forever changed. With factories concentrating on the needs of war, the entire population of the country found they could "make do" without new products. Rationing became a way of life and coupon books determined what wearing apparel was available and what menus could be planned based on what food was available. Children hadn't realized at the time that one popular dessert was really a way to not waste any milk by using it to make Junket, a milk-based pudding-like dessert made with sweetened milk and rennet.

More inspiring than what the factories produced and the rules of rationing, however, was the dedication of an entire generation, particularly the young men in uniform. Those who had their nurturing years embedded in this era saw such a spirit of national cooperation as being normal, and in a strange way, the World War II era is viewed as one of the most secure times in which to grow up in small town America. We were a nation of one mind and purpose.

Early in the decade, people's daily lives remained fairly routine in most towns and cities that were not populated by government offices. In the schools there was little discussion about war (or any other current event), as immediate news was not widely available and most parents and teachers were not comfortable with in-depth discussions of contemporary world events because of their own limited knowledge and their belief that children should not be troubled by what was happening outside their immediate experience.

Many homes at the time did not even subscribe to a city newspaper, only perhaps to a local weekly, such as "The Hummelstown Sun" or the "Middletown Press," the daily "Harrisburg Patriot" or "The Evening News," or "The Grit," a broadsheet aimed at rural and farming communities.

The same routineness of "business as usual" also was true to some degree with those serving in the military. While battles raged on the other side of the globe, military stationed in the states were generally out of touch with what was happening, as there was no way for them to know. There was no "transparency" for either military or civilians, mainly because there was no means by which to get "immediate" information on what battles were taking place where. What is notable is that, because they didn't know what was happening in far places, the typical enlisted man would perform his daily assigned duty, maybe watch a movie in a tented theatre or mess hall, or be writing letters home, oblivious to the battles "overseas."

In August 1941 the federal government had established the Office of Price Administration (OPA) and in May 1942 the OPA opened War Price and Rationing Boards in every county across America to monitor government-issued coupon books. Rationing of goods began almost immediately with ration books issued to both adults and children, regulating purchases in nearly every consumable. Families devised their menus around available food products and clothing purchases were limited to existing goods (which were few).

In the initial years of rationing, automobile owners had to turn in their tires at a collection station before ration cards were issued for replacements. However, as the war dragged on, rubber was so scarce that no new tires or recapped tires were available. If an automobile blew a tire and the owner had no spare, the car either sat out the war or the car owner would try to find a spare tire from a kind relative or neighbor. Many cars sat on blocks (for the lack of tires) for several years until the war ended.

By 1942 sixty percent of all civilian food items had been rationed, and hardship from the lack of goods was being felt in every corner. Everyone learned to re-use items rather than discarding them. Little girls who had mastered ironing skills by being permitted to practice on handkerchiefs were shown how to iron wrapping paper and ribbon so that it could be re-used. Hair curlers were fashioned from the covered wire closures that came on coffee bags. Children grew up thinking that people had always used this method to curl their hair once they outgrew rag curls.

Teen-agers in the 1940s had no luxuries because there weren't any. Even fabric for a prom gown was hard to come by, to say nothing of the scarcity of an escort for the event. Even so, a 1942 yearbook from a small town in central Pennsylvania described their prom in alluring terms, "The quiet charm of a rose garden inspired one of the most glamorous and bewitching proms ever held in our high school." What they didn't describe was that 75% of the attendees were female.

Reflective of the times, the same yearbook offered this dedication:

Through magic casements we Seniors of '42 dedicate this book:

To the boys of our class who are pledged to their country's service,

To the soldiers from our community and from all parts of our country who are adventuring for a new birth of freedom,

To our parents, our teachers, and our friends who are sacrificing so that liberty may not perish from this earth.

Based on the fact that news did not reach the bases any faster than it did to the general public—sometimes days after the event, it is unlikely that most enlisted men knew that on February 15, 1942, Great Britain had surrendered Singapore to the Japanese. This was a huge loss to the Allied Forces, but wasn't generally known for several days.

Then on February 23, the first Japanese "attack" on the American Mainland occurred—to the surprise of all—when a Japanese submarine surfaced near Santa Barbara, California. Imagine the initial panic to those who saw this happen, but it is quite possible that the men stationed in the training camps in other states didn't hear about this for days—and maybe not at all.

The Allied Forces were greatly outnumbered and, after believing that the lives of all of those in captivity on Corregidor in the Philippines would be endangered, General Wainwright ordered General Sharp to surrender his troops to the Japanese. This he did on May 10, 1942 based on two reasons: (1) he believed that the Japanese were fully capable of executing the 10,000 survivors of Corregidor and wanted to prevent such a slaughter and (2) he knew his forces would not be reinforced by the United States as had been previously thought.

For the Allied survivors this defeat in the Philippines was the beginning of three and a half years of harsh treatment, including atrocities like the Bataan Death March and the misery of Japanese prison camps, as well as the "Hell Ships" on which American and Allied men were sent to Japan to be used as labor in mines and factories. Thousands were crowded into the holds of Japanese ships, without sufficient water, food, or ventilation. Very few in the United States really understood just how terrible this was.

The difference between what was happening "on the war front" during these early years of the war and what was going on in the training camps is startling, maybe more so in hindsight than when it was happening. While it was understood that the recruits needed to be kept active with camping training and marching skills because they were being prepared to fight in the field, it is revealing to compare the "ordinariness" of the daily activities in the forts compared to life on the battlefields in both Europe and Asia.

This lack of information as to what was happening on the battle fields is astounding in hindsight. Because of delays in relaying information and the government's decision to not release any information to the public, families were left quite "in the dark" as to what their family members in the military were actually doing.

Further, once the troops were engaged in action, they were forbidden to reveal their specific location when they wrote letters home. While militarily necessary, this lack of information led to even more anxiety for the families back home.

November 26, 1942
Jefferson Barracks near St. Louis, MO

Following his enlistment in November, William H. Calhoon found himself on a bus that took him to St. Louis, a stranger in a strange land, particularly for someone who had never been outside of his home state of Pennsylvania. He had been sent to a training camp known as Jefferson Barracks that, while named for Thomas Jefferson, had none of the refinements of Monticello. Training camps were just what their names implied—places in which civilians began to become military men.

The oldest operating US Military Installation west of the Mississippi River, Jefferson Barracks was a major Reception Center for U.S. troops being drafted into the military during World War II. It also served as an important basic training site for the Army with billeting space for 13 officers and 1,500 enlisted men.

Basic Training by necessity is designed to be highly intense and challenging, both the physical training and the rapid psychological adjustment that is needed to become accustomed to an unfamiliar way of life. Basic Combat Training (BCT) is just that—basic. It is where individuals learn about the fundamentals of being a soldier, from combat techniques to the proper way to address a superior. BCT is also where individuals undergo rigorous physical training to prepare both mind and body for the eventual physical and mental strain of combat.

Most recruits would agree that one of the most difficult and essential lessons learned in Basic Training was self-discipline, as it was the first time many of these young men were required to meet a strict daily schedule with many various duties and to fulfill the high expectations for which most civilians were not ready.

All recruits were drilled in the basic elements of military life and trained to work as part of a team. They learned to operate and maintain weapons. They took tests to determine their talents and were taught more specialized skills. Paratroopers, anti-aircraft teams, desert troops, and other unique units received additional instruction at special training centers. Calhoon was early on identified as a candidate to become part of the military police. Two weeks later, Bill sent to his father a brief note on a post card—an important one—his new address at his next camp.

Dear Daddy,

My address is Pvt. Wm. A. Calhoon, CQE M.P. Bn, 7 Bldg. # 27, Fort Riley, Kansas.

> The Military Police served as the law enforcement branch of the Army, patrolling bases and local cities, investigating crimes, providing security forces and guarding POWs. In combat zones their primary task was directing traffic and providing information to men in search of specific units. MPs of a combat unit were generally well-regarded for manning their posts even under heavy artillery fire.

Fort Riley, Kansas

Upon arrival in Kansas, a place known by most of the young recruits as simply the setting for "The Wizard of Oz," was anything but the fantasy depicted in the movie. At Fort Riley, Bill Calhoon—and all of the other inductees—were stripped of the freedom and individuality they had enjoyed as civilians. They had to adapt to an entirely new way of living, one that involved routine inspections and strict military conduct, as well as rigorous physical and combat training. They were given identical haircuts, uniforms, and equipment, and were assigned to spartan barracks that afforded no privacy and little room for personal possessions.

A typical barracks

Bill wrote his first letter home after several weeks in training, particularly concentrated on the rudiments of becoming a military policeman.

December 1942
Fort Riley, Kansas

Dear Daddy,

I thought I would be out of here by now but here we are as yet. Some of our company shipped out last week and landed in Ft. Custer, Michigan. So I think by next Sunday we should be out of here.

We had our twenty-mile hike and that was about the longest twenty miles I ever walked. We carried full field pack including gas masks, rifles and bayonets. We walked about ten miles in two hours, then took a five minute rest and then walked ten more miles, came into our barrack and tore down our pack, cleaned our rifles, shed our shoes, then we ate, took a shower, and went to bed. It was two o'clock in the morning, we got up at six and took a two-mile march to get the stiffness out of our joints.

I am now a military policeman which is the best job in the Army. The guys that shipped out last week have two more weeks of training, then they get a furlough and report back for duty and get ready for business.

They told us that we should get a furlough as soon as we ship out to our permanent base. So at that rate I should be home in a month or two. I have had all my teeth fixed so I won't have to worry about toothache.

On Wed. and Sat. afternoons we play games, the favorite ones are volleyball and softball. We had started a league but since most of the games were canceled because of bad weather we had to break it up because some of the guys have shipped out.

It does not seem possible that we have been here seven weeks but we have. We have reviews all next week and so I guess we will be in our new camp in another week or two. As you know, we don't have mail now so I sure hope we get to a new camp quick.

Good-bye for now, Bill

December 30, 1942
Motor Convoy, Fort Riley, Kansas

Dear Daddy,

I am so busy I can't find time to write a letter so I will say I am O.K. and I like the Army fine now that I don't have to take so damn many shots.

Bill

On the Home Front

The war effort on the "Home Front" required sacrifices and cooperation, and raising an armed force was just one part of America's massive war effort. All of the armed forces had to be supplied with the uniforms, guns, tanks, ships, warplanes, and other weapons and equipment needed to fight. With its vast human and material resources, the United States had the potential to supply both itself and its allies. But first the American economy had to be converted to war production.

This effort brought immense changes to American life. As millions of men and women entered the service and production boomed, unemployment virtually disappeared. Millions of Americans left home to take jobs in war plants that sprang up around the nation. Economic output skyrocketed.

"Don't you know there's a war on?" was a common expression used with anyone who didn't seem to understand times had changed with being at war.

Americans learned to conserve vital resources. They lived with price controls, dealt with shortages of everything from nylon stockings to housing, and volunteered for jobs ranging from air raid warden to Red Cross worker.

Rationing became part of everyday life. For example, by 1943 full skirts, knife pleats, and patch pockets had been banned from manufacturing and shoes were not only rationed but also limited to six colors: black, white, navy blue, and three shades of brown—when they were available.

Meals for the most part, continuing even after the war

rationing was over, were unimaginative, but nourishing. It was typical in most households to have the same meal a particular day of the week, such as meat loaf, macaroni and cheese, creamed dried beef, hamburgers, scrambled eggs, chicken, or soup weekdays with hot dogs on Saturday and a pot roast on Sunday.

Canned goods soon were added to the list of rationed foods so that one not only had to wait in line, but also had to present a ration stamp for every food purchase. Then came the five percent "war effort" tax. A motto, "Use it up, wear it out, make it do, or do without" was coined to encourage the public to tolerate half a decade of rationing.

More encompassing, however, was the stock answer to almost every question as to how long the shortages and rationing, the blackouts and the boys being overseas, would continue. It was always the same: "For the duration." Everything, it seemed, was for the duration.[8]

Suddenly teenage boys were expected to be capable of victory on the battlefield. Even the term "boy" went from designating a male child to the honorable label as used in references such as "our boys over there."

Courses in high schools were streamlined to better prepare students to be useful for the armed forces and war industries. Commercial training turned more practical; military forms, nomenclature, rules, law and practices were emphasized; and a course named "pre-induction radio" (learning Morse code) flashed into popularity. In essence, the schools were preparing students for their part in a total war effort.

In the Military

After his training in St. Louis, Kansas, Bill was deployed and wasn't able to write home until a month after the letter he had sent from Kansas in December 20, 1942.

January 24, 1943
Fort Riley, Kansas

Dear Daddy,

Well, here it is already the 24th of January and my basic training is almost over and I will soon be at a permanent base.

Boy, was it cold out here last week. For this day it was between 20 and 25 degrees below zero with a forty-mile wind. I found out this week that after I get to a permanent camp I have a chance to go to school at Fort Custer to take lessons to become an instructor in rough and tumble fighting. It is a very tough but interesting course and means a longer time without getting a chance of promotion. But I will take it if I get a chance.

If you want to mail anything please mail it before Jan. 30, because after that it will probably have to be forwarded to me which means that it will take a long time to get there.

I have been officially notified I am now a military policeman and unless I get transferred I will be a M.P. for the duration. I am acting squad leader for our squad of rough and tumble fighters of our company. Our commander said that I must have done a lot of fighting in my time.

How did Eggie make out on his exam? I saw in the paper that they are still taking them left and right and they made some exceptions like for Dale Weaver.

Well, Daddy, I will tell you something that I am almost positive is true. There will be very few of us that do not get a chance of going to some kind of school which means a rating of some kind after you are through [and return to civilian life].

Last week we were quarantined because some kind of flu was going around and so we all had shots to fix us up so we would be immune against it, so we are fine again. There are more Pennsylvanians here than from any other place in the country.⁹ I believe it is because we are so smart! Did you think your son would ever be a policeman? Well, I am one and am proud to be one. When we get to our permanent camp I sure hope I will have time to write to everyone who I owe a letter to.

But here at the Replacement Training center we work on call by what is termed basic. But when we get through I am almost sure from what I saw of M.P.'s already that we will goldbrick a lot. All we will have to do is look nice and direct traffic and to shoot the shit which we do plenty of.

Boy, when it gets cold out here it really gets cold. There was one of the guards who stopped walking his post last Monday night and he froze to death so you can see that we stomp around out here.

Daddy, I wish you could go to church with me some Sunday out here just to see that the guys who are ready to die for their country go to church and pray to God and to sing His praises. If you could see it I know it would make you glad to know that the boys in the Army are full of church believers. They are not all drunks as some people would have you believe.

Will you please say hello to everyone for me and tell them I did not forget a one of them but I just don't have time to write. Tell Sis that I could show her how to wash dishes and peel spuds now.

So long, Your son, Bill

P.S. I hope Eggie gets in the M.P.'s if he has to come in the Army.

Trust in God and pray for a quick victory.

Please help Jerry to name our baby, will you? I can't think of a name to save my neck.

February 9, 1943
Postcard, "Setting the Rising Sun"

SETTING THE RISING "SUN"!

Dear Dad,

Here is what your boys are doing to the Japs and that is no kidding. I will write to you when we get to our new base.

Bill Cal....

This new base was to be Brookley Field in Mobile, Alabama which became the major Army Air Forces supply base for the Air Materiel Command in the southeastern United States and the Caribbean. Both Air Materiel and Technical Services Command organized mobile Depot

Groups at Brookley; then once the men were trained they were deployed around the world as Air Depot Groups, Depot Repair Squadrons, Quartermaster Squadrons, Ordnance Maintenance, Military Police, and many other units whose mission was to support the front-line combat units with depot-level maintenance for aircraft and logistical support to maintain their operations. This is the base where **Bill Calhoon was prepared on how to patrol installation areas in the Pacific Theatre.**

February 17, 1943
A comic post card with the phrase "Haven't Missed a Shot Yet!"

Dear Dad,

Just a card to tell you I am O.K. Hoping you are the same. Will drop you a few lines as soon as we get to our camp.

Your son, Bill Calhoon

March 7, 1943
Brookley Field, Mobile, Alabama

Dear Daddy and Sis,

Well, dad, last week we were out camping for four days. Then I pulled two straight days of duty and one day of KP so I didn't have much time to write. Now this week I am getting ready to help put on an Easter Sunrise service so I won't have much time to write. So please forgive me if my letters don't get home so often.

Well, daddy, it sure is hot down here in Mobile now. I am getting a swell tan on my face and hands. No kidding, it really gets hot as the devil down in Dixieland.

Well, daddy, I reckon I may be here for the duration. I think we are going to be attached to the 480th Air Base Squadron. We are now learning how to go out on town patrol in a jeep. We are also learning how to operate a two-way radio. We make out questions to ask prisoners. By the way, we still go to school twice a week.

About furloughs—they are not giving any except emergency furlough now. So I guess I will wait until Jerry goes to the hospital to get a furlough.

Gee, daddy, am I proud about the little sack of joy we are going to have next month. Hope it makes me so proud I won't know what to do.

Well, Daddy, I just can't seem to find a way to ask you, but as yet I don't know what the score on the orchard is. I know that Bowman must OK the mortgage, but if he does not approve it, what happens then?

I must get ready to close for this time because I must go to a law class.

So long, Bill

March 12, 1943
Brookley Field, Mobile, Alabama

Dear Daddy,

I am sorry I did not write last week, but we had a pretty busy week. We had three mock battles each of the last two days so you see we only had one day left and believe me I slept for sixteen hrs. and then went on guard duty.

I will get some pictures and souvenirs for you as soon as we get paid. You see I have not been paid since January 15 and am kind of low in funds. I have a camera but the damn thing doesn't work.

About all we do down here is loaf and drill. It rains almost every day. The weather is swell outside of that.

John Rider and those guys are about forty miles away from here so I am going to try to get a weekend pass and go to see them.

We expect to pull out in about six weeks. I think we are going to Alaska to guard the new highway.[10]

The mail is all screwed up down here. One day you get ten letters and the next day you don't get any. Jerry did not get any letters for a week and then she got eight letters at once.

I am not the official color-take-downer here at our base. We take the colors down[11] four nights a week.

Last week I saw a two-man sub of the Japs and I would not want to work in one of those babies. No kidding, Dad, they are only eight feet long.

Please send me Edgar's address as soon as you get it and I will give him the lowdown on Army life. I should soon be getting a furlough.

So long, Bill

March 17, 1943
Brookley Field, Mobile, Alabama

Dear Daddy,

Well, Daddy, we were to have furlough, but they were cancelled when we were alerted, so I guess we will be pulling out pretty quick.

The weather down here is pretty hot. About all we do is listen to lectures and do "close and extended order drill."

> Close and extended order drills are designed and practiced so that when the command is given, all of the men know exactly what to do. Close Order Drill, for example, is the precise method of marching in formation. Though no longer used to align combat formations on the battlefield, Close Order Drill still has several practical purposes. In addition to providing a standard, orderly manner for unit movements, it also teaches discipline, instills habits of precision and automatic response to orders, and ensures new team and squad leaders become accustomed to issuing proper commands assertively.

Since we have been alerted, we get up at 5:15 a.m. and work until 9 p.m. at night. We have one hour for chow at noon and one hour for chow at six p.m. The rest of the time we are working.

Gee, daddy, it takes six or eight weeks down here to get a picture made [likely he is referring to a formal military "portrait"] and that is longer than what we are going to stay here. So when we get to the next place I will try to get one made.

I am assigned to a motorcycle squad at the present, although right now we do more walking than riding! Honestly, I don't believe you ever get away from walking in the Army.

Jerry told me about the pigs. I sure hope you have luck with them.

I got a letter from Pud last week. I wrote to Eggie twice, but he has not answered yet.[12]

Well, dad, it is just about Easter. Down here in Brookley Field we are going to have an Easter sunrise service. I think it is going to be beautiful down here then. From the chapel you can look out over the bay and the sun rises out of the bay, so you can tell it will be beautiful.

Daddy, I am sorry about Easter cards. The night I was going downtown to get some more we were restricted to base. Now we can't leave the post, so I guess I won't be going downtown anymore so I can't get more cards.

I have some film now and I will take some snapshots and send them home.

So long, Bill

March 25, 1943
Brookley Field, Mobile, Alabama

Dear Daddy,

Well, Jerry has gone home so I guess I will get back to letter writing. Gee, it was swell to have her down for a week. Honestly, Dad, it was really wonderful to see her again.

I sure am glad to hear that Eggie is in the Air Corps.[13] In all honesty I did not think he would make it. But I believe that it will really build him up. I know that I look better and also feel better since I have been in. Jerry told me that I sure have a swell tan. She also told me that when I made love to her while she was down here that I could squeeze a lot harder than when I left. So you see the Army has done me some good also. I think Jerry is bringing some souvenirs home for you.

Well, Daddy, how are Larry and Barbara Ann? I know that by this time I bet Larry is really the boss up and down.

Next week is payday and I am going to have some pictures taken and I will send one home as soon as I can.

Well, I will close for this time and will write a few lines tomorrow.

So long, Your Son, Bill

P.S. The girls down here are all right.

March 26, 1943
Mobile, Alabama

Dear Daddy,

Boy, what a swell Easter day down here in Mobile. I did not see much of the sun in the morning because I was on guard Saturday night and slept until 12:30. But I was in church Sunday nite. Our chapel is right along Mobile Bay. We had all the windows open, there was a warm breeze blowing, the chapel was full of flowers and it was really swell.

Well, Daddy, how are the pigs coming along —also the garden? Gee, Dad, you know it would seem funny, but down here in Mobile we too are going to have our own victory garden. Of course, we may not be here to harvest everything, but some other soldiers will be here to take care of that part.

Well, only a few more weeks until that bundle of joy arrives over at my house. Gee, I am so proud to have a girl like Jerry for our children.

I just know I will never regret for a single moment I picked her to be my wife. Gee, Dad, I am telling you she is the sweetest little girl in all the world.

Well, Daddy, there's not much to say except, "we'll keep 'em flying." So long, Bill

March 28, 1943
Government Street Presbyterian Church
Mobile, Alabama

Dear Daddy,

Well, Daddy, you should be down here in Mobile today. I have on my sun tan and still I am very warm. As you can see I am writing this letter in the Government Street Church. So I guess I will try to tell you about the church U.S.O. here. They have one in every church in Mobile and since they are all alike, this will go for anyone of them.

They have a kitchen in them with an icebox. No kidding, Dad, you can go anytime and help yourself to anything that is in it. Then there is a room such as I am in now to write letters and also a game room in which you can play pool or anything you wish. They also have a reading room where you can read. So you see they are all run by the U.S.O. which is one swell organization.[14]

Well, Daddy, I wish I could describe the day for you; it is really swell out. The sun has been shining all day and the weather is super.

We get paid on Wednesday so I will come to town next week and have some pictures taken. I promise to send you one.

I am glad to hear that Eggy is in the Air Corps. He told me he likes it out in Utah. I have lost his address, so will you please send his address to me. By the way, I think you will have to put my serial number on my address pretty soon so as soon as I find out for sure I will let you know.

I have Jerry's camera now and soon hope to take some snapshots to send home.

Boy, it was swell to have Jerry come down for a week. It was almost like having a furlough except that she is the only one I saw, but anyway it was swell. I am not kidding you, it was better than swell.

Well, Daddy, I am going out and raid the ice box now, so I will say "so long" for this time.

Your son, Bill

51

P.S. I think Jerry will have twins by the way she looked when she was down. Say "Hello" to everyone for me.

What Bill does not mention in the letter to his father is that he earned the following military qualification in May 1943: **M1 Rifle Marksman (M1 Rifle MKM 171).** The M1 was a .30 caliber, semiautomatic weapon, standard issue American rifle used from 1936 through 1957. General George S. Patton, Jr., called it, "...the greatest battle implement ever devised."

The following appears to be the last letter Bill sent from Mobile Alabama as he mentions "this nice spring day," muses that he may run into Edgar in San Francisco when he (Bill) ships out, notes that his father should visit Mobile, and that he is eager for the birth of his son, which we are assuming is wishful thinking as there was no test at that time to determine the sex of the baby in vitro.

May 16, 1943
Mobile, Alabama

Hi, Pappy,

How is the old man this nice spring day? (Are you still going out to see Rosie?)

Well, I see where Edgar has made Pvt. How

do you like that? I see also where he has been transferred to San Francisco. Maybe I will come across him. Boy, that's right! John Rider has made it too. I see he is in New York. Well, he had better get himself a furlough and marry Winnie before some Private gets her.

Pap, how do you like the way Sud and his pals are kicking the shit out of those would-be German soldiers?

Pap, you should come down here some time on vacation. The sun would do you a lot of good.

Is Cal still goldbricking in at the post? How are the hogs? Boy, there should be a lot of fat there for you sometime this winter.

Daddy, please forgive me for not writing more often.

That son of mine soon better make his appearance or else I will be gray-haired from excitement. Boy, am I going to teach him to take women out as soon as he can talk! Gee, dad, no kidding. I am all excited about it, no lie.

Well, I have to hit the sack fast, so I say so long for now.

So Long, Your son, Bill

The above letter can be described as "upbeat" and positive, with the imminent birth of Bill's son (again presuming here that the baby's gender could only be guessed), teasing his father, hoping to see his brother, and with no foreshadowing of his heading into the New Guinea campaign (that had begun in January 1942 and lasted until the end of the war in August 1945) of the Pacific Theatre.

May 24, 1943

[This letter was likely written in temporary quarters, waiting to ship out.]

Hi, Daddy,

I am now in California. We had a swell trip coming out, but still when we got here we were pretty glad to get out of the rain. I can't go to see Eggie yet. I think I may get a chance if we stay in Calif. long enough.

I haven't heard from Jerry, so I think she must be in the hospital.

Well, Dad, I reckon we won't have as much fun from here on, but I must say I had a swell time in Mobile.

I got a letter from Pud last Sunday and as soon as I can get some V-Mail to use I am going to write to him.

How are the pigs coming along? How is the victory garden growing?

They were right when they said that the southern sunshine is here. Boy, hot! I think in about another week I will be baked and cracked, too. Here we are waiting to go to the combat zone and they have us doing a lot of close order drilling.

Well, Dad, I reckon we should not have too bad a time except for the hot weather. We have swell movie theatres. Out here the theatres are named for army stations; for example, Number 1 theatre is named Bataan, and so on. We also have two companies of WAACs out here. Most of them are from the East. We talked to two from New Jersey and three from New York.

Well, Dad, we have some clothing to be issued yet and it is as hot as hell, so I reckon I will close for this time.

So long, Bill

May 26, 1943
U. S. Army

Dear Daddy,

I am not going to be stationed here [place name removed, but likely in or near San Francisco]. I can't tell you whether I am going overseas or not. This seems to be a pretty swell place if only I had time to get around. I can't even get to see Eggie at the present. I may be able to do so later on.

Boy, do we have work! No kidding, dad, I can't tell you what we do, but I sure can say we work.

I guess by the time this war is over Clam [Clarence] and George will be in the Army. That will be a pretty swell record for you. Five sons in the Army.

Daddy, I reckon that son of mine is not so far off. I can only wait to hear whether it is a boy or girl. From what Jerry says, it may be two!

I know Eggie is a member of the bedpan commandos, but I must admit they do a pretty swell job.

I got a letter from Helen yesterday and from what she says, Barbara Ann must be a regular little corker.

Jerry told me that John Rider is in New York and that he, too, has in the first sleeper.[15] I reckon with the exception of me, the guys from Hilltop[16] are making out all right.

Daddy, when we leave here we will have a new A.P.O. When you get a card from the government with my new A.P.O. on it you will *then know I have reached my new destination.*

Daddy, whenever possible, please use V-Mail. If I do get overseas it will speed the mail up and even if I stay here in the U.S., it will get here quicker.

So long, Bill

It is likely that Bill's unit deployed from the San Francisco Port of Embarkation (or possibly its subsidiary Oakland Army Terminal), as during World War II, more than 4,000 voyages by freighters and over 800 by troopships emanated from there. This Port of Embarkation carried nearly 1,650,000 soldiers and 23,600,000 ship tons of cargo to support the efforts of General MacArthur in the Southwest Pacific Area and Admiral Chester Nimitz, Commander in Chief of the Pacific Ocean Area.[17]

Unfortunately the records of ships used to carry troops to their theatres of operations were destroyed intentionally in 1951. According to U.S. National Archives, in 1951 the Department of the Army destroyed all passenger lists, manifests, logs of vessels, and troop movement files of United States Army Transports for World War II. There is no longer an official record of who sailed on what ship.[18]

The Date of Departure for Bill's unit was May 30, 1943, the day before his son was born (although he could not have known that at the time). The Date of Arrival was June 23, 1943. The destination: The Western Pacific Theater of Operations— somewhere in the Pacific Ocean area, the likes of which Private Calhoon had never seen.

World War II: July 1943–December 1943
New Guinea

The New Guinea Campaign of the Pacific Theatre lasted from January 1942 until the end of the war in August 1945; thus, William Calhoon would be arriving on the Pacific front lines at about the midpoint (1943) of this very long campaign in the Philippines.

Bill would be one of the 620,845 men being transported to the Pacific Theatre in 1943 alone. As the men boarded their troop ship in San Francisco in May 1943 they had had no real experience with any part of battle war. Particularly, there would have been no foreshadowing that Calhoon's unit would be a part of the New Guinea campaign of the Pacific War that later was described as **"... arguably the most arduous fought by any Allied troops during World War II."** [1]

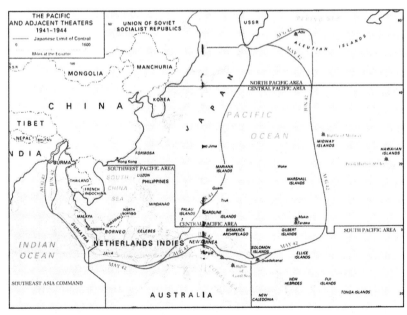

The Philippines

Most of the men who had had their stateside training in Alabama would have little idea of where New Guinea was located, let alone how close it was to Australia. Originally an outpost of the British government, in 1905-1906 the New Guinea citizenry was told that the responsibility for its governance was being transferred by Britain to Australia.

During World War I Australian forces had seized German New Guinea and in 1920 (following WWI) the island was deemed to be administered by Australia under a League of Nations mandate. All of these islands then became known collectively as the Territories of Papua and New Guinea until February 1942 when they were invaded by the Empire of Japan.

From the time in the late 1930s that the United States government first believed it would be playing a major part in what would become World War II, the Philippine Islands were considered to be of great strategic importance because their potential capture by Japan would pose a significant threat to the U.S. through its western coast (California). Therefore, by October 1941 the United States had stationed 135,000 U.S. troops and 227 aircraft in the Philippines as a safeguard.

When Luzon—the largest island in the Philippines and 15th largest island in the world—was captured by the Imperial Japanese forces in 1942 during their campaign to seize the Philippines, this action became a real threat to the interests of the United States and its Allies.

A few months after Japan's takeover, General Douglas MacArthur—who was in charge of the defense of the Philippines at the time—stood staunch—and vocal—in his belief that it was imperative for the safety of the United States to recapture the Philippines from the Japanese. This idea was opposed by the U.S. Pacific Commander Admiral Chester Nimitz and Chief of Naval Operations Admiral Ernest King who both argued that the drive to regain the Philippines should wait until they felt that victory would be certain.

Japan particularly was interested in holding the colonial capital on the south coast of Papua. The Japanese military viewed it as the strategic key, believing that capturing its main port, Port Moresby, would both neutralize the Allies' principal forward base as well as serve as a springboard for the Japanese invasion of Australia, should they choose to do so. For these same reasons General Douglas MacArthur, Supreme Commander Allied Forces South West Pacific Area, was determined to hold Luzon.

However, on March 11, 1942, eight months prior to even the military enlistment of William Calhoon far away in Pennsylvania, General Douglas MacArthur unexpectedly was ordered by President Franklin D. Roosevelt to abandon the island fortress of Corregidor, located at the entrance of Manila Bay in the southwestern part of Luzon Island, all part of the Philippines. To be left behind at Corregidor and on the Bataan Peninsula were 90,000 American and Filipino troops, who, lacking food, supplies, and support, would soon succumb to the Japanese offensive.

General MacArthur did not want to leave the Philippines, but obeyed his orders, leaving his house, property, and personal possessions there on the islands. With his departure, the Imperial Japanese Army concentrated their efforts on the island of Corregidor where Lt. General Jonathan Wainwright had taken command on Corregidor and had placed Major General Edward P. King in command of the troops on Bataan.

General Wainwright at first refused to surrender to Japan even though the island was relentlessly pummeled by the Imperial Japanese artillery for several weeks. It was then surrounded and cut off from receiving any reinforcements and supplies from the United States. Wainwright was trapped.

Bataan fell in April 1942 and, without being able to obtain Wainwright's approval, King was forced to surrender his Bataan troops to the Japanese.

On the night of May 5, 1942 the Japanese landed troops and tanks. They quickly began advancing towards the Malinta Tunnel which had been dug through solid rock and offered complete protection from artillery or air attack. Command communications and medical units were located there, including many patients and nurses and an underground hospital with a 1,000 bed capacity.

To avoid a massacre, Wainwright was forced to surrender the troops on Corregidor and the other three fortified islands. This meant there were approximately 15,000 more Americans and Filipinos who had laid down their arms and were totally defenseless at this point on Corregidor. They were captured, the Philippine Islands were lost, and the U.S. Joint Chiefs of Staff had no immediate plans for their liberation.

Lt. General Wainwright had tried to communicate to the other islands to also surrender, by broadcasting the following message on the Manila radio station KZRH:

TO: Major General William F. Sharp Jr.

After leaving General (Masahara) Homma with no agreement between us, I decided to accept, in the name of humanity, his proposal and tendered at midnight, tonight 6-7 May 1942 to the senior Japanese officer on Corregidor the formal surrender of all American and Filipino armed troops in the Philippine Islands. You will, therefore, be guided accordingly and will, I repeat, will surrender all troops under your command both in the Visayan Islands and Mindanao to the proper Japanese officer. This decision, on my part, was forced on me by circumstances beyond my control. Let me emphasize that there must be on your part no thought of disregarding these instructions. Failure to fully and honestly carry them out can have only the most disastrous results.

However, the Imperial Japanese General Masahara Homma refused Wainwright's offer of surrender and 70,000 American and Filipino soldiers captured there were forced to undertake what would be a death march in which at least 7,000 military men and women perished.

At the same time, the Visayan Islands and Mindanao were commanded by General Sharp who was directly under General MacArthur and, to confuse matters, the American-Filipino troops on the outer islands were getting conflicting messages from General MacArthur. MacArthur did not want these islands to surrender but wanted Sharp to create guerrilla units and hide in the hills (which did happen to some extent by those who escaped the death march early on its route). Finally Colonel Traywick, Wainwright's emissary, reached General Sharp to express the severity of the situation where eventually the U.S. commanders on the Visayan Islands, Mindanao, and Cebu surrendered.

Skirmishes and battles continued into the next year and in August 1943 the leaders of the Allied nations agreed to a change in strategy. The intense campaign resulted in a crushing defeat and very heavy losses for the Empire of Japan, even though most of the Japanese troops did not come into contact with Allied forces, instead being cut off and subjected to a very effective blockade by the United States Navy.

Staying Connected

"Our Boys"

On his troop ship headed for New Guinea, it is unlikely that Pvt. Calhoon and his mates would have heard much of what was happening in the Philippines, only that they were headed to the islands and would presumably be stationed there, perhaps for the duration. The duration, of course, would have its own problems which face all wars—how to keep the troops engaged and their morale up. The key was to "keep the home fires burning" and the men connected to that home fire.

Homesickness and Staying Connected to Family

Difficult as it may seem to those living in the 21st Century, homesickness has long been recognized as a specific military disease which can lead to desertions, sickness, and death. During the Civil War, Union Army bands were sometimes forbidden from playing "Home, Sweet Home" and it is said that more than 5,000 of the men (74 of whom died) were diagnosed with what then was termed "nostalgia."

Until the time of World War II homesickness was considered a disease that, if not cured, could be fatal. It continued to be a concern, if not termed a disease, during WWII because it was recognized that soldiers were particularly susceptible to homesickness and some of them deserted in part because they missed home so much. Military physicians and leaders viewed this homesickness as capable of enough harm to impair seriously an army's efficiency. This is why processes were established to keep the soldiers busy with drills and work assignments as well as providing recreation and other activities to keep them occupied.

At the Front 1942–1945

With nearly every country in the world affected by WWII, more than 100 million soldiers fought on three continents. Many fought in places they had never seen and in some cases, had never heard of, such as the Philippines, Guadalcanal, and Iwo Jima, not to mention Luzon and Leyte. Families taped up world maps on their living room walls and used them to follow the course of the war as they listened to wartime radio reports or read newspaper stories. In that way in the letters they wrote to the military personnel, families could refer to places with some knowledge at least of the location.

For the soldiers in far-off places—many away from home for the first time in their lives—any reminder of home was a comfort. For example, in 1942, while building the Alaska Highway through the vast Yukon Territory, a homesick soldier, Carl K. Lindley, erected a sign pointing the way to his hometown of Danville, Illinois. On the sign, he included the distance—2,226 miles!

Many soldiers served even farther away from home, including the Philippines where soldiers were as much as **10,000 miles** away from home. Direction signs like these were a common sight wherever U.S. soldiers served. These signposts acted as small reminders of home—reminders of what the men were fighting for.

Thus, the military took seriously the prevention of homesickness and kept the men busy on and off duty, provided recreation, showed movies (where possible), and, in more urban areas, relied on the USO. However, the major effort was expended in encouraging the soldiers and their families to write letters.

The Importance of Mail

It often has been said that for members of the armed forces the importance of mail —particularly during WWII —was second only to the importance of food.[2] The emotional power of letters was enhanced by the fear of loss felt by the troops (both from the war and from family events) and the strong need for communication with family during times of separation.

In the worst case, letters from a father, husband, son, or brother killed in battle or missing in action might be the only lasting connection between the soldier and his family. In addition, the constant lurking danger and all of the uncertainties of war placed added emphasis on letter writing as the only means by which most servicemen and their families could stay connected.

Military personnel have expressed that they felt the most connected to their homes and families through letters. Thus, those on the home front were encouraged to write about even the most mundane events and basic activities—daily routines, family news, local events and persons, even hearsay—all of which helped to keep the armed forces linked to their communities. The men were encouraged to write regularly about feelings and thoughts that for most men were normally expressed only at home and on special occasions. The military recognized the importance of writing regularly to assure devotion from both the writer and the reader.

Bill Calhoon took this expectation seriously—more so than did his brother Edgar who three decades later told his own son who was entering the service that he (the son) didn't have to write home. Edgar told the young man that when he (Edgar) was in the service he was ordered by the army to write every week and he hated it. "Write only if there is something I need to know," was Edgar's instruction to his son. As this book was being written, the son recalled that some years later, when the two were driving to a golf course, his dad had told him stories from his days in the military. The son recently expressed that he wished he had recorded the stories at the time since he did not have any letters from his father as his cousins did from theirs.

Love Letters

It became a given that the essential connector—direct and personal—between those in the military and "the girl back home" was letters. Thus, the military service made it a priority to develop a process that would support and encourage love letter-writing.

Government, social agencies, and community organizations all worked for sweethearts and spouses separated by oceans to stay in touch through mail, and there was a very strong emphasis in the camp culture to stay connected to family and friends back home. In some units arrangement for assistance was made for those who might have been semi-literate or even had illegible handwriting.

USOs also offered services to help the men write letters home to families and girlfriends, and officers reminded the enlisted men to "write home," knowing how important this was for morale. It also was not unheard of for officers to write to families to encourage those who were not writing to their enlistees to begin to send letters to them.

Such efforts to keep America's troops informed about home life—hopefully with some degree of detail—allowed the men to be in the war while maintaining a critical link back to their families. Some servicemen also wrote to friends they knew, or to girls whose introduction was made by a buddy or a helpful family member, to develop new relationships and fight off loneliness.[3]

Victory Mail

Victory Mail, known as V-Mail, was a system established so that more letters could be sent home effectively from those in service. V-Mail used standardized stationery, but added a microfilm process that resulted overall in a total of lighter, smaller cargo (to allot more space in the planes for other war supplies) that would ensure that more letters could reach military personnel around the world.

For example, a reel of 16mm microfilm could contain 18,000 letters (and for every 150,000 letters microfilmed, over a ton of shipping space was gained) and take up only a fraction of the space that would be needed to ship paper letters. The military men (and women) would write on standardized paper provided to them, the letters would be photographed, placed in microfilm, and mailed to the States where they would be reprinted with envelopes, then addressed and mailed.

As an example, 12 million letters were V-Mailed in just one month in June 1943. (Those not familiar with the process[4] found themselves wondering how these men could write their letters so carefully on this very thin paper without tearing it before it arrived in the United States.)

The use of V-Mail was aided by news reports showing—usually through newsreels such as "The March of Time"—how these letters were processed and sped along to the military personnel. V-Mail was further promoted as patriotic with advertisements emphasizing contributions to the "War Effort," such as the saving of cargo space, but, more importantly, to lift the spirits of both military personnel and civilians.

Advertisements also helped to increase the number of letters written, including letters from neighbors and friends—all who felt inspired to help brighten the day of a soldier. Letters also were written by pastors, church members, scout masters, teachers, and school principals—all realizing the importance of mail and wanting to do their part for the troops. It certainly was an extraordinary time of common effort, the likes of which has not been seen at any other time in history.

Of course, the drawback in promoting letter writing is that all correspondence in both directions had to be censored lest sensitive information be unwittingly conveyed. Thus, while the military and their families were strongly encouraged by the government to engage in correspondence with those in service, that correspondence needed to be secured. This censoring, in addition to the orders they had been given, is the reason why so many servicemen's letters dwell more on the mundane than on how they were preparing for or engaging in skirmishes and battles.

Some families didn't realize that the soldiers had to be careful about what they wrote in their letters and probably wanted to ask the men to write letters that were more specific to what they were doing, but the families were so glad to hear from the servicemen that most didn't want to ask.

An example of simple censoring as shown below; sensitive words were simply blacked out.

want that ████to have it before ████. You can tell them I am in North Africa but nothing further, I think, about my work here. Also you could tell them I was in Ireland and England last year but not much more than that about my stay there.
   I think I've done pretty well to be a lieutenant colonel at 31, just 9 months after I received my majority. Col.████, the Ordnance Officer, has been well satisfied with my work I guess as has also Gen.████, t e Base commander. Gen.████ has been transferred to another place and I was sorry to see him go. He told me the other day he wished he could have been here long enough to have presented me with my promotion but that was not to be. I knew him in North Ireland and England when he was a colonel and was chief of staff of the old organization I was in. He succeeded Col.████, who was transferred from the unit last summer.

Those who were careful not to name names of places and officers were still at a loss sometimes as to how to "fill" a written page with information that was not about sensitive matters. Those at home who received the letters were often frustrated and disappointed to find the information in letters written home was rather humdrum and frequently repetitive.

Wives and parents could do little more than wait and worry as they followed the news, not really aware that much of it was being censored. However, no one would want to put the country in danger by allowing the military personnel to write about where they were, what missions they were part of, or perhaps just how difficult daily life was, so everyone worked hard to write letters that were positive and as "newsy" as possible, and without complaint.

Regardless of what was written in the letters, those at home were grateful to receive any mail from the front and many kindly mailmen would make an extra home delivery, in addition to the regularly scheduled twice-a-day service, if a letter arrived at the post office from a serviceman to his family.

For a time the overseas military personnel were limited to writing only two letters a week until the V-mail system was refined. Bill explains to his father in the first letter he wrote once the troops were quartered in July 1943 after Bill had been in New Guinea for several weeks.

V-MAIL
July 13, 1943
New Guinea, South West Pacific

Dear Daddy,

Well, Pappy, I guess you have waited a long time to get a letter from me. I will try to tell you why I have not written.

You see, due to a long process of censoring we are allowed only two letters a week, so I have been writing my two per week to Jerry. However, it may be soon that we are allowed five a week, and that may solve my problem.

I am sorry that I did not get to the office to hunt up Eggie. The nearest I got was when we got aboard the ship to come over. That was about *twelve miles from Frisco.*

As to your question about the women, I have seen only two since I got here. Both of them are nurses that happened to go past in a jeep.

[After addressing his father's questions implied by his own answers, Bill provides his own measured, yet poignant, comments in not being the first to know about the birth of a son, his first child.]

I guess you knew before I did about the baby. I did not hear until June 24.

[However, Bill continues in stride by commenting about the war and his brother Francis (Pud) who was serving in the European Theatre.]

I guess Pud is now running the Germans back to Berlin. We have started to send the Japs back to Tokyo, too.

[Bill closes with this affecting wish....]

It won't be long now until I see my son.

So long, Daddy, Bill

Five weeks later Bill writes a cheerful letter to his father about general conditions, as much as he can relay, and he implies a longing to be home by mentioning the fresh tomatoes and green beans from the family garden. His letter ends with a request to his father and well-wishes to his friends with a touch of longing for home.

Particular note should be made about William's devotion in writing to his father, because it had to be difficult to keep up a correspondence when anything about the war that one would want to say could be classified and censored.

August 3, 1943
New Guinea

Hi, Pappy,

Well, I'm not having a lot of time to work in or not much time to write in. No longer do I look at the women who look nice. Rather, I look at about ten thousand ants per hour and no companies of men lined up for retreat, but rather companies of mosquitoes who line up at dusk to battle through the mosquito netting that we sleep under.

But, Dad, that is what takes the cake. Now we have cots to lie on and we put our mosquito net up and sleep inside of the net with just a pair of shorts on and let the mosquitoes buzz around and we can hear the cursing because they can't get at you.

Boy, it's hot down here. It is winter now and it's hotter than it ever gets back in the States. And rain, well, you have never seen rain until you see it rain down here. At night it is darker than the inside of a cow.

We must have about a million different kinds of insects down here. Boy, do they go to work on your hide.

I reckon when I get back to the States I will sit down and get me a good cold glass of water and take all day drinking it. I have not even heard of cold water since we left the States.

So long for now, Bill

August 12, 1943
New Guinea

Dear Daddy,

I guess it is high time to write and tell you all about New Guinea. Well, first it is hot, boy, and how! It was winter time when we got here; even then it was 110 degrees. Imagine 110 in the winter time! In about a month the rainy season will start. The soldiers who were here last rainy season said that it pours down—sometimes for days at a time. I hope we are not here for more than one rainy season.

Even now we have rains like I have never seen. Yet they are what they call showers. Last week the ground was covered with about four inches of rain, yet it was only a shower.

74

Dark! When the sun goes down, it gets as dark as the inside of a cow.

Please send me Pud's serial no. and A.P.O. so when I am not too busy I can write. I will try to make this a long letter so if I am too busy to write for a few days you will be able to excuse me for not writing.

I got a letter from Miss Shultz [their neighbor] the other day so I guess I will have to answer her.

I see where Pud and the rest of the army did a swell job in Africa. They are not doing so bad over there now. [This is in reference to Pud's being part of the North Africa Invasion which ended in May 13, 1943.]

Jerry tells me you are spoiling Billy for us. Well, Daddy, since I can't be there to spoil him I guess everyone else is doing their share.

There is a shortage of writing paper over here so I guess I will have to use V-Mail for a while yet.

I guess everyone over that way is married by this time. I sure hope they have as happy a marriage as Jerry and I do. We have not lived married life long, but when I get back we are going to make up for it.

I received the "Middletown Press" the other

day. It was dated May 1st, but it seemed new to me. It was swell to read about the old hometown and how everyone back there is.

I got a letter from Mr. Johnson, our high school principal.

Well, it is time to go to work, so I will say So Long for this time.

Bill

Samuel A.
Johnston

Principal,
Middletown
High School
1941

Middletown High School Building
Blue and Gold, 1941

August 17, 1943
New Guinea

In the following letter which refers to being "on the road" to Tokyo, the plan in the Pacific was just that, to rout the Japanese out of the islands of the Pacific, then go north to Japan. This following letter would be as strong a statement a soldier would be able to make without the letter's being censored.

Hi, Pappy,

Well, I finally found some paper so I will write a good letter for a change instead of a V-Mail post card greeting. Well, Pappy, we are now on the road to Tokyo; it is a long tough road but we are finally on the way.

I am now having spring fever, the warm days of about 112 degrees really give me the spring fever and it makes me feel kind of lazy.

I got a letter from Pud and he told me to tell you I have heard from him. He thought I was in Mobile yet. Will he be surprised when he gets the answer telling him I am in New Guinea!

[The following is in reference to the "victory gardens" that families were encouraged to maintain because of the scarcity and rationing of food. Further, those in the military rarely saw any fresh food and developed an intense longing for it.]

Boy, I sure would like to eat some of the tomatoes that you are picking about this time. Or the same fresh green beans; boy, I am going to live on fresh vegetables when I get back. I have eaten enough canned chow to last me for two lifetimes.

I sure think that Billy must be spoiled by now. Jerry says he won't be quiet unless someone is making a fuss over him.

There are some guys from the 104th California National Guard over here if I can just find out where they are.

Daddy, how are chances of getting some plug chewing tobacco and sending it to me? It sure comes in swell to work or stand guard when it is raining day and night, which it does a lot.

Pappy, will you tell Doll and Clam and John and Elizabeth I asked about them? I am too busy right now to write each of them a letter, or perhaps when we are not quite as busy I will be able to write.

Tell Bill Rider and Don Miller to write and let me know how they are making out with the women.

Daddy, I am safe enough, so please tell everyone I am OK. Healthy and still kicking, but it sure will be swell to see Jerry and Billy and all of you at home.

So Long, Bill

The Southwest Pacific
September 4, 1943

Hi, Pappy,

Well, Pappy, I imagine you would enjoy the weather if you were down here for the winter. That is, it is winter back in the States, or fall. Down here it is spring.

Boy, what a warm spring day we had with temperatures anywhere from 98 to 112 degrees, so you can imagine it gets quite warm in the summer.

How is the garden? I'll bet you really had some swell tomatoes. Boy, could I go for a big tomato sandwich right now. When are you going to butcher the hogs? Maybe if you wait awhile I will be home to help you.

Pappy, I had the very bad luck to see some of the South Sea women. Boy, what liars the movie shows are. The kind you see down here are black, they wear no sarongs and they can't dance! I don't know how the Asian women are, but I may take time out to see.

I think by the time I get home I won't even know what you mean when you say a dollar.[5] I am now fully aware of what pounds, half-pounds, florins, and shillings are, but I am forgetting what dimes, nickels, and quarters are. When Billy says, "Daddy, give me a quarter," I will probably say, "Here's a florin, Bud."

Well, Pappy, I can't tell you where I am or what I am doing, but I can say I am O.K, healthy and happy, if you can be happy in the jungle.

So long, Your son, Bill

Southwest Pacific
September 18, 1943

Hi, Pappy,

It is now getting to be spring down here in the S.W.P. and what a spring it threatens to be. Hot days, so hot you can do nothing but sit around and sweat them out.

We had some swell entertainers from the States over here about three weeks ago. Ray Bolger and Little Jack Little were here in person. Boy, what a time we had with him. He is one of radio's top comedians today and he sure lived up to his fame that night. In about five minutes he had everyone from the Col. on down laughing.

There were three guys who were here about six weeks ago; they were tops, too! Then last night we had a guy from the Metropolitan Opera Company here. He did not sing high class stuff; he sang old and new favorites. His partner played an accordion which he could make talk.

I got a letter from Pud last week. It was dated June 16 so you see it took a little while for it to get here. I had written to him twice yet he said that so far he had not heard from me. It takes air mail about 30 days to get here.

It was 118 in the shade today, not bad for a winter day, heh?

Pappy, I think I will be afraid of women by the time I see one again.

God Bless you and keep you.

So long, Bill

Southwest Pacific
September 21, 1943

Hi, Pappy,

Well, it is still getting hotter every day and life is about the same as always.

I got seven letters yesterday and none today, so you can see the mail is kind of screwed up.

I got a letter from the young people down at our church and, boy, what a gang of them are getting married. It was really a swell letter. Each one of them wrote a few lines. I also got four letters from Jerry and two from Miss Shultz.

Thanks a million for the swell card. Is there any chance of sending me some film? The number is 127. I could really take some fine pictures here.

I haven't heard from Pud or Eggie, but I guess I will get an answer one of these fine days. God Bless you and best of luck.

So long, Bill

Many of the letters sent home by the soldiers expressed a longing for familiar meals and individual favorite foods, especially anything that was "fresh out of the garden." Even families who didn't normally plant vegetables found themselves trying to garden because many items were not available in grocery stores and what was available was expensive. Further, there was a campaign in the states for families to grow their own food as a sign of patriotism as well as necessity, since the government commandeered a major percentage of homegrown produce previously raised to sell at markets.

While rationing of meat had begun early in 1942, a crisis during the 1942-1943 winter saw butchers' display cases in the

States gradually emptied of meat. Steak was the first to disappear and soon not even hamburger was to be found in most meat counters in the East, as the government had requisitioned 60% of prime and choice cuts and 80% of utility cuts. It is estimated that much of the remaining beef flowed into "the black market" (a term first coined in occupied France in 1940). Even Spam, a canned meat made up mostly of ham scraps, was found among the items rationed beginning in February 1943.

Those on the home front who had the space and the skill to raise pigs and chickens had begun to do so. This was a relatively new venture for the Calhoons, but something Bill's father "Pappy" saw as needed. It is unlikely that they considered "raising" beef, but relied on what small livestock could be managed in the back yard.

Many larger communities established community gardens where individual families each had its own section. Both individual and community victory gardens continued to flourish throughout the war, reaching an estimated 20,000,000 at its peak, and producing 20 percent of all vegetables grown in the United States. This also allowed for more of the commercially grown vegetables for use by the military.

A Little on the Lonely Side

Another arena that helped both the military and "the girls they left behind"—with sometimes years separating the couple—was the music of the period. With WWII being the centerpiece of the 1940s decade, American popular music became the popular music of World War II, even though as a genre, the World War II songs started even before the United States became involved in the war with "The Last Time I Saw Paris," which was written after the fall of France in 1940.

When on December 7, 1941 the United States officially became part of what would become World War II, the newly composed songs "Remember Pearl Harbor" and "We Did It Before and We Can Do It Again" were recorded only days after the attack. Throughout the war, songs followed events with unusual rapidity, with the public singing along shortly after hearing the songs on the radio.

The military services had their traditional songs with "Anchors Aweigh," "The Marines' Hymn," and "The Caissons Go Rolling Along," but the Army Air Corps initially had none. That problem was solved in 1939 with the song whose opening lines became familiar to the whole country: "Off We Go into the Wild Blue Yonder."

Among all the music written during the wartime there were any number of patriotic songs specific to this country and to each branch of the service; however, in a class by itself was "God Bless America" which struck the strongest chord (second only to the national anthem) among both the military and civilians, particularly when sung by the full-throated, unforgettable voice of Kate Smith.

With so many eligible men out of circulation, the songs of the time helped to formalize and direct the sentiments of American womanhood who had much to lament. Some of the song lyrics were complaints such as "No Love, No Nothin' (Until My Baby Comes Home)" and "They're Either Too Young or Too Old." Other songs allowed any number of women to bewail that they "Don't Get Around Much Anymore." If some women fretted that "Saturday Night Is the Loneliest Night of the Week," others professed that "You Can't Say No to a Soldier."

Some servicemen, of course, worried about the constancy of their wives and girlfriends back home and many songs reflect that concern. Examples include "Somebody Else Is Taking My Place" and "Everybody Knew but Me;" however, the best-known song on this theme was "Don't Sit under the Apple Tree with Anyone Else but Me" which was wildly popular because of its message to "stay true."

A sampling of the multitude of popular tunes written between 1939 and 1945 includes the following:

A Fellow on a Furlough

As Time Goes By

Bell Bottom Trousers

G'Bye Now

Goodnight, Wherever You Are

Happiness is Just a Thing Called Joe

He Wears a Pair of Silver Wings

He's Home for a Little While

I'll Be Back in a Year, Little Darlin'

I'll Pray for You

Johnny Doughboy

Miss You

Say a Prayer for the Boys Over There

Silver Wings in the Moonlight

Song of the Seabees

This is the Army, Mr. Jones

'Til Reveille

Till Then

Until Tomorrow

Waitin' For the Train to Come In

We'll Meet Again

White Cliffs of Dover

Wartime romances had to adjust to long distances and many couples planned their marriages and weddings during military furloughs and, of course, babies were born while their fathers were away at the battlefront, which was case with the child of Bill and Jerry Calhoon.

Hollywood rose to the occasion of war adventures and romances, producing (in short order) a series of films with war themes. Those released in 1943 included the following of many hastily put together "war movies" of this year:

For Whom the Bell Tolls – Humphrey Bogart and Ingrid Bergman

Sahara – Humphrey Bogart and Lloyd Bridges

A Guy Named Joe – Spencer Tracy and Irene Dunne

Action in the North Atlantic – Humphrey Bogart

Aerial Gunner – Robert Mitchum

Air Force – Gig Young

Appointment in Berlin – George Sanders

Background to Danger – George Raft and Sidney Greenstreet

Bataan – Robert Taylor

Destination Tokyo – Cary Grant and John Garfield

Edge of Darkness – Anne Sheridan and Errol Flynn

Guadalcanal Diary – Preston Foster, Lloyd Nolan

Spitfire – Leslie Howard and David Niven

They Came to Blow Up America – George Sanders

This Land is Mine – Charles Laughton and Maureen O'Hara

(Note the dearth of female leads in these movies.)

While light reading predominated in the States in early 1942, it wasn't until later in the year that books about America's fighting men began to appear and it was 1943 before they were widely distributed. Even though many of the novels were heavily censored so as not to expose any military to danger and they conveyed only glimpses of the real trials of combat, the novels were popular because of the huge interest in the war.

The more important and most popular books published in 1943 included *They Were Expendable, Guadalcanal Diary, Into the Valley,* and Marion Hargrove's *See Here, Private Hargrove,* a humorous account of the author's own war experiences. A favorite of many readers was Lloyd C. Douglas' *The Robe,* a story of the life of Christ, and by 1945 this book had sold 2,000,000 copies. Not surprising, however, the best seller of the year was the *Red Cross First Aid Manual.*

Paperback books, first introduced in 1939, increased in sales during the war years and the Armed Services Edition program published cheap paperbacks of a size that would fit in a man's pocket. At the height of the program 40 titles a month were being sent out to the various military bases and, throughout the war, around 100,000,000 copies of these paperbacks were distributed free to servicemen.

Southwest Pacific
October 12, 1943

Hi, Pappy,

Uncle Sam has been hooking me on mail lately. I haven't had any for three days now; so I sure hope he makes it tomorrow.

It now rains almost every day. When it is not raining the sun burns you up, so I will surely appreciate some cold weather when next I come in contact with it.

I think I asked you in my last letter, but in case I haven't, will you please send me a pipe? I can't buy one over here for love nor money. Don't buy a good one, just any old kind will do. It will probably last me until I get to Australia to buy myself one. I think we should get a rest leave in about January or February.

I still haven't heard from Pud since I moved to my new A.P.O.

Pappy, will you tell Jerry in case I forgot to renew my subscription for the "Middletown Press?" It runs out in December. I want to tell her every day when I write but I forget it.

I think I know where Bill Rider[7] is stationed. Someday when I get a chance I will hunt him up.

Pappy, how much do Jerry and I owe on the orchard?

Well, Pappy, I must get some shut-eye so I will say God Bless you and keep you.

Bill, Your Son

V-MAIL
October 31, 1943

Hi, Pappy,

Just a few lines to let you know I am still alive and kicking.

Billy will soon be six months old and that is how long I have been in foreign services.

The natives are getting whiter⁵ every day. I received a letter from Clam and also Doll just before Clam went in the Navy. I sure hope he finds himself a good job in the Navy. I also received a letter from Eggy last week. It looks as though he will be stationed in Alexandria for a while.

Pap, I am sure you would enjoy all the hot weather we are having down here. Life down here is hot with never a cool day. Take it easy, Pappy.

As ever, Bill

By November 1943 another bleak holiday season loomed "in the States" as nearly every American family had one of its members "away in the war." Christmas catalogues were restricted in number of pages allotted to them and many items were stamped with the words, "Sorry, not available." Thus, even those who had money found that many items could not be purchased. Parents became ever-increasingly creative in finding gifts for the children, as little ones struggled to understand that Santa could not produce items tagged in the catalogue or newspaper ads as "Unavailable."

When one of a series of government Limitation and Conservation Orders prohibited the use of traditional toy materials such as steel, tin, rubber, and lead, manufacturers substituted cardboard and wooden toys. Cardboard and wood were not as enduring as the original materials, but at least the substitution was ingenious enough so that children would not be completely disappointed on Christmas morning.

It was an odd, somewhat tense time because servicemen were all over the globe: families did not know when they would be coming home, no real plans could be made for anything, children grew up without their fathers, mothers had to make do on the meagre military pay of their husbands in service, or find work. Many mothers and children moved in with the parents of the mother or the father. Jerry Calhoon and her baby son Billy lived with Jerry's parents for the duration. Everything, it seemed, was for the duration.

Civilians for the most part continued to write positive, upbeat letters to ensure that the person in service would not have to worry about things "back home" and the servicemen did the same about the dangers they faced, and for the same reason. In many ways, life was just put "on hold" near the end of 1943, with everyone waiting "for the duration."

V-MAIL Service
November 9, 1943

Again we see the attempts by Bill to sound positive in what he wrote. Like most service men, he counted the days, talked about the weather in New Guinea, asked about the livestock, indicated missing the hunting season in Pennsylvania, mentioned the weather back home, reminisced about ice skating with the coming winter season, and even risked a mild comment about the war. The benedictory closing is touching.

Dear Pappy,

Today I have one day over a year in the service. I also have 18 days to go until I have six months in foreign service. I think that is pretty good; how about you?

It rains night and day here. The sun is out sometimes. When it comes out it burns you up so I really don't mind the rain.

Have you butchered the hogs yet? I guess you will get no rabbit and squirrel this year. But I believe that next year we may be hunting again. How is the weather? I hope it is not too cold. Is it good ice skating there as yet?

Well, Pappy, things are looking better over this way. It has been a bitter fight. There are a lot more bitter fights coming, but at long last I think we are finally finding the road to Tokyo and Tojo.

God Bless You and keep you, Bill

November 25, 1943

Dear Sis,

Thank you for forwarding that letter to me.

Jerry tells me how swell it is to see you now and then. She says you build up her morale. Boy, would I like to see Billy, Barbara, and Larry all at the same time. Sis, the natives are getting just a little lighter in color. Say Hi to Larry for me.

God Bless you and keep you, Sis, Bill

New Guinea
November 25, 1943

Bill's offering a reassuring comment on the Thanksgiving feast in the far distant Pacific set the tone for this letter. A likely meaning of Bill's phrase which he has used before is that the residents of the Philippines were becoming "Americanized" (more white)[9]. Also apparent is that Jerry needed more money than what Bill's allotment could cover, and that she found child care from her own mother for Billy so that she herself could take a job.

Hi, Pappy,

Boy, did Uncle Sambo treat us guys swell today! We had turkey, sweet potatoes, pickles, cranberry sauce and candy. We had ham for chow tonight so Uncle Sam took good care of his boys in the Southwest Pacific all right.

Pappy, if you get a check for me for back pay from Hershey, will you tell me so I can let the union know about it.

So Flash Miller has cracked up his car. Boy, that is just what I thought he would do.

As for Clint Smith's bitching, someday I am going to ask him how he would like to be over here fighting with Tojo.

I am glad Clam likes it in the Navy. Give me his address and I will write him a letter.

Give me Eggie's address and I will drop him a line, too. I got two letters from Miss Shultz last week and once more Winnie was back to ask me why they had to keep John from coming home more often.[10]

Have you killed the hogs yet?

Jerry told me she would like to come over to see you but she can't make it since she is working down at Hershey Dept. Store.

Well, Pappy, Tojo has gotten a little more headway on his way back to Tokyo and it will be a great day when we pin him clear back.

God Bless you and Best of Luck, Bill

One day later Bill sends his Christmas "card" with a short message.

November 26, 1943
Postcard, "Christmas Greetings"

This is about the only kind of Christmas card we have, but, Pappy, I do wish you a very Merry Christmas and a New Year in which we might meet.

Your son,

So long, Bill

New Guinea
December 15, 1943

Hi, Pappy,

Well, only ten more days until Christmas. So far there is no sight of ice on the creek here so I guess I will have to be satisfied with going swimming.

Pappy, I made a swell souvenir for you. I worked on it about three months, then found out I could not send it home. I have started another one which I know I can send home, so whenever I finish it I will send it to you.

We are going to have a Christmas service on Christmas Eve, that is, if Tojo doesn't interfere too much so as to make it impossible. The way it looks now, though, we don't have much to worry about.

How is Larry doing? Still bad as ever? I got a letter from Edgar last week. He says the southern women are all right. I see where Bill and Matt Rider are about to meet in Australia.

I am expecting a rest leave to Australia any day now, so perhaps I can pick up something for you from Down Under.

Good Luck and God Bless You,

Bill

Bill wasted no time in thanking his father for the items he had asked him to send. Noting that "Jello will taste super" is most indicative of the typical meal fare of mainly C rations. [11]

The US also developed a lighter weight ration—identified as K ration—that was intended as an emergency ration. The K ration was not well-balanced nutritionally and provided fewer calories, about 3,000 calories for three meals compared to 6,000 calories in C rations. K rations also included four cigarettes instead of the nine cigarettes included per meal of C rations. In spite of being intended to be eaten for limited periods, US and Allied troops did subsist on C and K rations for long periods of time, especially in remote areas that were difficult to supply, even when out of combat.

Bill also notes that he expects to be going to Australia for a rest leave. Likely there were no furloughs to the States because of the distance and, most certainly, because of the lack of transportation. Certainly there would be no extra space on a carrier. The last two paragraphs here are a summary of Bill's missing home, and the letter closes with a reminder that he is limited in what he can say in writing—the only means of communication at the time.

New Guinea
December 18, 1943

Hi, Pappy,

Thanks for the swell package. Got it today. Boy, that chewing gum and candy is really swell. The Jello is going to taste super.

I got a Christmas card from Aunt Bert[12] today. She had her return address on the envelope so I will be able to write to her.

Got a letter from Eggie last week. Found

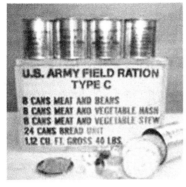

out too that a guy from Hummelstown who came in the army with me is stationed in Australia near where I expect to go for a rest leave.[13]

He took some snapshots and when I get them from Australia, I will send one home.

Received a letter from Bill Rider the day before yesterday. He was telling me about hunting. Boy, would it be swell to go hunting again.

Pappy, Life is getting boring over here. Nothing to do but eat, sleep, and work. In church today we sang Christmas carols. Did that ever take me back home! Pappy, I can't say much more.

God Bless you and Good Luck, Bill

New Guinea
December 18, 1943

Dear Sis,

Sis, how are chances of sending me some magazines?

Boy, singing Christmas carols sure took me back

to the young people's meetings at church when we used to go caroling. Honest, Sis, I can't tell you what I do or anything about what you say or even anything about the weather. So I can't find anything to write about. Please forgive me for such a short letter. I will try to write more next time.

Good Luck and God Bless You, Bill

A month would pass before Bill's family would receive his next letter.

Importantly, rumors that had begun as far back as April 1942 became more believable that General MacArthur had begun to train, organize, plan for, and lead his Southwest Pacific Command through New Guinea, New Britain, the Bismarcks[14], and Morotai[15] in preparation for a major attack on the Japanese in the Philippines. All of the Allied military waited with the proverbial baited breath.

Interlude

— Tales from the Home Front: December 1942–April 1945 —

Many behind-the-scenes activities and events, in addition to direct support for the war, impacted or were impacted by the War. Some of these events were isolated incidents occurring in various parts of the United States and some were the united effort of all 48 states.

Hershey Bars

It is generally known that the Hershey Chocolate Company played a key role in supporting the war effort during World War II. In fact, the Hershey plant devoted the bulk of its chocolate production to the military, with the civilians taking second place (those who were children during the war years well remember that Hershey bars were scarce and were considered a "treasure" when one discovered a store that had them on the counter or in the display case). Of course, no one complained that the bulk of the candy was being sent to the troops.

Hershey Chocolate Company was responsible for the development and production of what was known as the Ration D bar, created as a survival ration that provided subsistence calories and nutrition to soldiers facing extreme conditions. One of the most important features of the candy was that the chocolate did not melt. This is the chocolate bar remembered by most enlisted men who later reported at home that "the Hershey bars we had didn't even melt."

In fact, some years later Bill Calhoon's twin daughters remember their dad talking about these Hershey chocolate bars, confirming that they just could not be melted even when the men tried putting them in their metal helmets and heating them over a campfire. Bill likely shared with his comrades that he had worked at the Hershey plant, but at that time they weren't making these special bars for the hot climate of the Pacific war zone.

In addition to the production of this special chocolate in its town factory, Hershey—like other American communities— also responded patriotically to war time conditions. In the town of Hershey nearly everyone was mobilized for the civilian war effort. Most adult citizens took training classes that were related to that effort and many volunteered for duties such as taking two-hour shifts on the aircraft warning signal service that was operated round-the-clock. At first, the aircraft warning station was mounted on top of one of the cupolas at the Hotel Hershey. However, once the hotel became the internment location for the Vichy French (see below) the warning station moved to one of the towers at the nearby Milton Hershey School Senior Hall.

The Vichy French and Hershey, 1942-1943

Not many people knew that during the War the Vichy French government was being sheltered in Hershey, Pennsylvania, at the Hotel Hershey, three miles from Hummelstown. While some area citizens would, of course, know about the presence of this group, the information was held in confidence, and even those who worked at the Hotel were not completely sure who these "Vichy French" were and what they were doing here in the United States near the state capital of Pennsylvania. However, they trusted that the U.S. government had a good reason for housing these foreigners in the grand hotel perched on the high hill that could be seen from the peaks of South Hanover Township—which abutted the hotel grounds.

So who were these Vichy French who had come from France and were, in a sense, refugees, but of a class protected by the American government? And why would a group sympathetic to the Germans even be allowed on American soil?

The long journey (and story) of these Vichy French families had begun in the spring of 1940 when Germany invaded and defeated France. The German conquerors, for whatever reason, had left a large portion of southwestern France unoccupied, and it was in this area (specifically in the town of Vichy) that a new French government, sympathetic to the Nazi regime, was established.

This government officially became known as the Vichy French and, as part of political protocol, the Vichy government sent an ambassador to the United States. Some questions were raised as to whether the United States should recognize any government of Nazi-occupied France, but, by some decision, recognition was granted.

By late 1942, however, the United States had lost patience with the pro-Nazi French government and, after Germany arrested American diplomatic personnel in France, the United States responded by arresting the pro-German Vichy government ambassador and his staff who were serving in the United States. However, the government found itself in an awkward position and quickly needed to find a place to at least temporarily house this diplomatic party.

The Hotel Hershey was chosen to sequester these Vichy French government representatives for several reasons: Hershey Estates was co-operative; the accommodations were of high quality and, possibly most important, the Hotel was in a secluded and defensible location. (As diplomats in a very strange situation, these Vichy French were under both the rule and the hospitality of the United States.)

By early evening November 17, 1942, the French Ambassador and 91 other various officials from across the United States and their families arrived via automobile caravans for their internment in Hershey, to remain as guests of the United States federal government. Most Hershey residents were unaware that the Hotel was being used as a detention site even though a fence was put up around the Hotel and carefully guarded after the installation.

During the several months of what amounted to an elegant house arrest, most of these Vichy French officials declared their allegiance to the Free French Government and were allowed to leave the Hotel and seek political asylum in the United States. On September 30, 1943, the Vichy French internees departed and on October 1, the Hotel reopened to the general public.

Local citizens who were employees of the Hotel at the time were expected to be discrete and most were, aware that these guests assured their employment, since the Hotel might otherwise have closed based on the fact that few people were vacationing during the war. As might be imaged, however, some employees did have interesting tales to tell.

Financing WWII: The Impact of War Bonds, 1942–1945

In 1942 the United States held its first War Bond Drive, fully realizing that the U.S. Treasury could not bear the entire cost of a major war. World War II eventually would cost the United States $300 billion dollars, twice as much during the war alone as it had spent in its entire existence before the war, with the federal budget rising from $9 billion in 1939 to $98 billion in 1945.

At first taxes were increased with an additional 5 percent Victory Tax. To assure payment of this tax, in June 1943 the government approved the first automatic deduction of taxes from paychecks. But this tax still was not enough to finance a war. More cash was needed and bonds sold to the public could be a vehicle by which to channel cash into bond purchases, thus helping to prevent inflation. While the rate of return was below market value, bonds were recognized as a stable investment and aided the war effort, as well as meeting the emotional need of the general citizenry to help the War Effort.

Defense Bonds first went on the market on May 1, 1941 and were renamed War Bonds after the US entered the war in December 1941. These bonds were designed to be affordable for everyone, beginning with stamps costing 10 cents; these were popular with children who could insert these stamps into special "books." When a book had been filled to the amount of $18.75, they could be redeemed for a $25 bond in the future. Bill's daughter Janet recalls that even into the 1950s when she was in elementary school they were continuing the savings stamp program but by the late 1950s the banks initiated a program by which children still brought their money into school where it was placed into a savings account at the local bank.

In addition, an emotional advertising campaign—greatly boosted by a series of War Loan Drives (also called Bond Rallies)—brought in even more needed money. These Rallies were very popular, with those in cities featuring Hollywood stars speaking, singing, or just being present. In towns, local talent was recruited to attract a wide audience.

Bond Rally in Pennsylvania, 1943

Eight War Loan Drives were conducted from 1942 to 1945. Each was meant to raise an additional $9-$15 billion in sales. Towns were assigned quotas, with the aim of promoting competition between towns. Volunteers went door-to-door, pleading for sales and rewarding purchasers with stickers showing support for the cause to display on their window or door.

Posters were also used effectively to appeal to the public. For example one popular poster showed a wounded soldier on a battlefield asking the question, "Doing all you can, brother?" Another showed a smiling pilot in flight with several U.S. fighter planes in the background with the caption, "You buy 'em, We'll fly 'em!" (http://www.rare-posters.com/ww2bond.html)

Japanese War Balloons over the United States, 1944–1945

Between November 1944 and April 1945, Japan launched 9,000 "balloon bombs" against the United States, providing an opportunity to justify to any doubters that the Civil Defense program was important. These bombs were carried by balloons sent from the east side of Japan transported by the trade winds—set to explode in various locations in the United States 40 hours after launching.

Most of the balloons fell harmlessly into the Pacific Ocean, but more than 300 of the white spheres made the 5,000-mile Pacific crossing and were spotted fluttering in the skies over western United States and Canada—from Holy Cross, Alaska to Nogales, Arizona, and Grand Rapids, Michigan.

In March 1945, one balloon even hit a high-tension power line and caused a temporary blackout at the Hanford, Washington plant that was producing plutonium that would be used in the atomic bomb dropped on Nagasaki five months later. The farthest east any bomb traveled was to Maryland, but it did not explode. More of the balloon bombs landed in the southwest desert of the United States where they exploded but did no damage. There are rumors of the death of one family in the mid-west from such an explosion. The government, however, did not release reports on the incidents so the Japanese would not know if their mission had been successful and, likely, would not repeat the balloon bombs.[1]

The bombs caused little damage, although their potential for destruction and fires was large. The bombs also had a potential psychological effect on the American people. Thus the press did not publish any of the balloon bomb incidents. The closest the Japanese came to success was that one of the balloons descended near the Manhattan's Project in Washington State. This balloon caused a short circuit in the powerlines supplying electricity for the reactor cooling pumps, but backup safety devices restored power almost immediately.

U.S. military regularly shot the balloons out of the sky, but enforced the policy of absolute secrecy to deny the Japanese any news. The news media cooperated with the military and this silence was so successful that even today few people have heard of these bombs.

A Harsh Winter at Home, 1944-1945

During the winter of 1944-45, the bitterest in years, an acute fuel shortage left Americans in the eastern half of the country shivering in their homes. Overburdened railroads, manpower shortages, and blizzards were to blame. A brown-out was ordered throughout the nation, and the use of neon signs[2] was prohibited. Stores closed at dusk. Throughout the East Coast some schools were closed for lack of fuel. Businesses went on short weeks. Downtown shopping areas in cities were empty and dark at night and a midnight curfew was imposed on bars and nightclubs.

Families were affected by rising costs for the coal most of them still used to heat their homes. Many whose heating systems had pipes only to the first floor, counting on a dispersal system though a ceiling vent to heat the second floor, vowed they would install new systems following the war.

However, what made everything more bearable was that some of the troops at that time were beginning to come home.

World War II: 1944

Most who lived during the period of history known as World War II would agree that there was something greater than each individual, connecting all of us, both in the mission and in the daily events of life.

During this time the nation was immersed in the war or the war effort on every level and at every age. Even those too young to understand the war felt a connection to the community and to something they were a part of. Of course, those younger than teen-age weren't cognitively aware that this was anything unusual. They just assumed that this was typical life, with its energy and commitment. All who lived in the community and larger country were viewed as simply family in one way or another.

The scope of the national involvement is best reflected in the numbers: 12 million in uniform, war production at 44% of the GNP, almost 19 million more workers than there had been five years earlier, with 35% of them women. The nation was immersed in the war effort on every level.

This was a generation of servicemen who, when they later came home from service, made no demands of homage from the generation that followed them, even though the nation prospered economically, politically, and culturally because of the sacrifices of those who served.

In sum, this "Greatest Generation" would later be viewed as one of towering achievements whose membership respected and viscerally understood just how many others of their generation with whom they had served did not make it home from the war.

=====On the Home Front 1944: "It's for the Duration!"=====

By 1944 everyone was "hunkered down" for the duration. There were hints that the Allies would not lose this war, but without guarantees of total victory, rationing with its accompanying shortages of goods and services increased in severity, making a "normal" life difficult. There was even a shortage of alarm clocks and in some factory towns roomers found their clocks missing.

Millions of Americans relied on the radio as their primary source of war news and by 1944 NBC was devoting 20 percent of its airtime to news, compared with 3.6 percent in 1939, while 30 percent of the airtime at CBS was given over to the news. With so many men overseas (more than 16 million Americans served in the armed forces during WWII), America's wartime industry relied heavily on women to keep up its frenetic pace. Between 1940 and 1944 the number of employed women rose from 12 million to 18.2 million[1] and at the height of the war years, women made up more than one-third of the civilian workforce (while millions more served as volunteers in the war effort).

College enrollments throughout this time also reflected the paucity of young men, and during 1944, for example, more than 80 percent of the journalism school graduates were women. The campus population was decimated by the draft and there were no college deferments in those days (except, at the discretion of the local draft board, for a young man to complete an academic year). Some colleges dropped football entirely for a season or so. On the other hand, the two service academies at Annapolis and West Point—especially the latter—emerged as the wartime sports powerhouses and in 1944 Army dominated the national football scene, winning all eighteen of its games by lopsided scores during that period, defeating Navy by the closest score of their season, 23-7.[2]

However, as 1944 was gearing up for the biggest challenges yet, those on the home front saw the war as dragging on through the routines of daily living. The federal amusement tax (such as on movie theatre prices) was raised from 10 to 20 percent while the cost of living rose almost 30 percent. Wages, for the most part, were frozen, and the result was a further necessity to "tighten the belt." In addition to the victory surcharge that had been initiated the previous year on purchased goods, a new victory tax of 3.75 percent was imposed on income. Life was not easy on any front.

Scarcity of goods continued—and in some areas increased—with shortages of candy, ice cream, and chewing gum, as well as meat, butter, fats, and canned goods. Even though America's farms, orchards, pastures, and ranges were producing record amounts of vegetables and meats, the Lend-Lease Act[3] and Armed Forces' needs added an increment of 25-50 percent to a civilian demand already swollen by increased purchasing power.

By early 1944 shipping overseas of canned goods had increased in amounts approaching one-half the entire production of the United States. To the dismay of smokers, cigarette rationing was also introduced that year. Rubber sneakers were impossible to buy and people had to use shoes with reclaimed rubber soles that left ugly black marks on almost any floor surface. All, from mothers to janitors, were dismayed at the difficulty of removing these marks.

The wildly popular singer Kate Smith[4] went on a successful marathon tour selling war bonds, and all across the country people continued to collect scrap metal and newspapers. Iron, steel, rubber, nylon stockings, and cooking grease were also collected, as well as tin cans whose tops had been removed by a can opener so that the cylinder of the can could be stomped flat. (Contests were held in schools to increase the number of tin cans collected and flattened, although the younger children were not permitted to risk cutting themselves with this latter task). Households were asked to save tinfoil, string, and toothpaste tubes along with the tin cans. One of the unusual items asked for was rubber bathing caps even though they could not be recycled; the bathing caps were one of several items on the collection list only as part of the war effort to engage the entire country—and it did.

Continuing these and other routine traditions was one way the adults kept life as normal as possible for the children in the face of the stark reality of the ever-present war. Wives and parents could do little more than wait and worry and follow the news, trying to imagine what their loved ones were going through. In their letters home, some husbands found ways to code their whereabouts, such as mentioning the time of day that their wives could then interpret as longitude and latitude. Every family eagerly watched the mail for letters, which offered at least a temporary reassurance of the writer's safety. On the other hand, everyone dreaded an unexpected knock at the door announcing the delivery of a telegram that began, "We regret to inform you. . . ."

Automobiles ceased to be used for pleasure because of gas rationing, and the unavailability of replacement parts for cars led to their not being driven unless necessary.

One thing that was most plentiful was letters!

V-Mail (Overseas)
January 21, 1944

Hi, Pappy,

Boy, what chow we get on D.S.[5] We have the best chow I have had since I left the states.

Time goes fast up here. The weather is hotter than it was back at 503. [See explanation following this letter.] But the nights are cool and so you can sleep like a log. We pull six days of night work and six days of day duty. The bad thing of night turn is you must pull 2 hours at night.

I have learned to drive a jeep. There are two guys to a jeep which is not bad. In fact I like it very well. I think by the time I get back I may be able to drive an eight-wheel truck. I learned to ride a motorcycle back in the states. However, I would not risk one over here for a Master Sergeant rating. You can't get air mail envelopes up here so I will have to use V-MAIL until I can get some air mail.

Well, pappy, can't say much more today. I will try to write tomorrow again.

God bless you.

Bill

Note: This number 503 and other similar three digit numbers are the numbers for Army Post Offices (APO's) and Fleet Post Offices (FPO's) used during WW II as a Post Office for military units in a certain area. Each Army Post Office was issued a specific number in a similar way to the Australian Postcodes and U.S. Zip codes used today. 503 was the APO for Base B, Oro Bay, New Guinea.

January 31, 1944
New Guinea

Hi, Pappy,

Today I have been overseas 8 months. Billy is 8 months old. Quite a day.

I am sorry about having to use V-Mail. But since I have been up here on St. S. from back at 503 I have not been able to get air mail envelopes. So I have this V-Mail.

Jerry told me that it was nice and cool back home for Christmas. Boy, what a contrast. It was really warm over here. Right around 125 if I remember correctly.

We have a visit from Tojo about 5:30 every morning. He comes over just in time to wake us up for chow; usually he does not bring calling cards along with him. However, every now and then he lets us know he is still in the war.

But whenever he comes he finds us in a fox hole which means he can drop all the calling cards he wants and he won't get any personnel anyway. He does hit something worthwhile every now and then. But not often; he is a pretty poor shot. Boy, you sure can't say much on one of these notes. Don't worry, Pop. We are taking care of Tojo. That is the truth.

Bill

Beginning in April 1942 and continuing to October 1944 on the front lines, General MacArthur trained, organized, planned for, and led his Southwest Pacific Command through New Guinea, New Britain, the Bismarcks, and Morotai in preparation for a major attack on the Japanese in the Philippines.

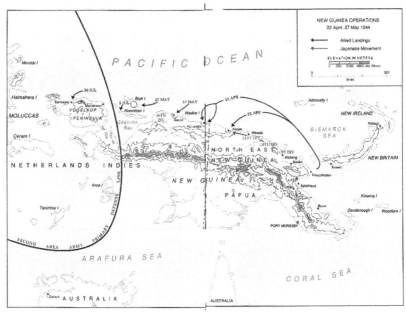

February 9, 1944
Philippine Islands
APO 321

(Mindoro, Philippines)
It appears that Bill's unit was moved.

Hi Pappy, Sis, and Helen,

Today I baked my first cake. It's tonight rather. It looks good, but I will have to wait until tomorrow to find out if the guys like it. I ate a piece myself and as yet I am not sick.

Yesterday I played my first game of ball in the Philippines. We lost two to nothing. I did not even get a hit. In fact, I struck out twice and flied out once.

We had ice cream the day before yesterday and I mean to tell you it hit the spot.

I guess we really went to town here in the Philippines. Hey, I don't know why the Nips[7] want to burn Manila.[8] But you can bet your sweet life they are going to pay dearly for that.

Speaking of ball playing, the ball diamond here is the best I have seen since I left the states. All you need to make a diamond is a road grader. Then you just have to go over it a few times and it's like a board. There is no sickle

grass to knock down or coral to move.

But what I like best about this place is that there are no air raids. I mean none at all. Boy, it's really swell not to have any raids.

Right now I think we are having it the easiest since we left Frisco back in '43. I guess it won't last long, but it's swell while it lasts.

As yet I have not gotten any Christmas package. Don't have any idea when we will get it.

If you see Miss Shultz tell her as yet I have not gotten her Christmas package. Tell her I will write as soon as I get more envelopes. Envelopes are mighty scarce right now.

You know, Pappy, this old war may wind up in '45. I mean we are really putting the clips to the Nips. The guys in Europe are doing pretty fine, too.

Hope I get a chance to get to see reconciliation come true.

Your son, Bill

February 12, 1944
New Guinea

Hi, Pappy,

I got paid yesterday—six pounds, 19 shillings, and nine pence. Fortunately there was a little pence in it, so I am sending it along for a keepsake.

Gee, Pap, I don't know what to write about so it will be a short letter.

Almost nine months I have been here. It doesn't seem possible but it's so. I only hope the work might go so fast. Believe me, Pappy, the more work you do and the more excitement there is, the faster time goes.

When we landed in Port Moresby in June it was kind of hot down there and then when we got to 503 it was hot there, too. But then it got easier. Now we have been here at 322 where it is kind of warm and we work our asses off and time is once more flying.

I am sweating out a watch from Jerry now. It should get here sometime between now and May.

Honest, Pappy, I can't find anything more to write about, so I will sign off for now.

Good luck and God Bless You, Bill

February 14, 1944
New Guinea

Dear Sis,

Boy, you are just about an old maid now, aren't you? Anyway, Sis, Happy Birthday. I am sorry I could not get a Valentine or a birthday card. Here we don't have such things.

One thing, however, the Red Cross gives us plenty of stationery. Back at 503 they used to try to sell it to us.

Thank you for the knife you gave Jerry to send to me.

How is Larry doing these days? Has Jerry been over lately? She told me that you finally got some snow. Boy, that white snow must really be beautiful. Just like a pretty woman, I'll bet.

No more news for this time.

Good Luck, Sis, Bill

Sometime in February 1944

Hi, Pappy,

How are you and Rosie making out? You know spring is just around the corner back there, so you ought to get on the ball.

117

I am sending along a bracelet for Sis. Maybe she will have to get a link or two taken out. It's something I made in my spare time.

Gee, Pap, except to tell you all that we are finally beating Tojo every time he moves, I can't say much for this jungle over here. Boy, I hope either and if we move again that we move out of the jungles. I would like to see a house for a change.

Pappy, did you ever eat C-rations? Boy, don't ever go on a diet comprised of them. They say they are good for you. If they are, I wish I had something that is bad for you every now and then.

John Rider is getting married in June if he makes it home before he is given a boat ride. Boy, he got a good deal. He has been in the States for about 14 months now. I hear Dale Weaver is getting draft fever. He is afraid his friends and neighbors are going to catch up with him.

Don't take any wooden nickels, Pappy.

Bill

February 14, 1944

—No place noted, Red Cross letterhead

Hi, Pappy,

Valentine's greetings from Guinea. Boy, things are a little warm here, but I think Tojo feels the hurt worse than we do.

Jerry tells me that Billy's teeth are coming through finally. That is a relief. She said she got a walker for him. She is going to sell the baby carriage. I think I will tell her to keep it for a few years yet. What do you think?

It will probably take a long time for this letter to get to you because I am sending it free as I have no airmail envelopes or our mail stamps.

I wrote to Bud about two weeks ago, but I guess it will take anywhere from two to 2 ½ months for him to get it.[10]

I am also sending a florin along with this letter.

Good Luck, Bill

February 26, 1944
New Guinea

Hi, Pappy,

Gee, I'm sorry I did not write to you twice last week. I promise not to do it again.

I got a letter from Pud last week dated November 15. Quite a long time to get here, but, anyway, he was making out O.K. He should be sweating out his relief to come home by this time. As yet they have not decided how long you must be over here before you get relief leave. I hope it's not over two years. It is 18 months in Africa. That is plenty long to be away from the good old U.S.A. and that is no lie. You never miss the States until you leave them.

It's not the big things you miss over here in the jungle. It's always the little things that are hard on you. Like hot and cold water. The water over here is all the same. When you drink it, it's too warm, not hot enough to make showering and taking a bath a pleasure; however, you get used to it.

The day I get out I am going to put on a white shirt, my white slacks I got married in and eat a gallon of ice cream. What a day that will be! Pappy, I have a lot of things to catch

120

up with, so be on the lookout when I get home.

Pappy, Jerry was afraid to ask you so will you please tell her how much we owe on the orchard. Please, Pappy, you have not sold it to Slim, have you? Will we be able to get a clear deed too when we get it paid off? I just would like to know because some day Jerry and I want to build a home there. So, please, Pappy, take care of it until I get a chance at it, will you? Thanks for everything, Pappy.

Your son, Bill

APO 322, Unit 1
New Guinea
March 13, 1944
Serial Number 33244300

Hi, Pappy,

Well, old boy, how are you and Rosey making out these days?

Pappy, I had ice cream — today. The first time since I left the States. It tasted like something from heaven. It was made in Australia. I don't know how they got it clear up here, but there it was, so who am I to worry how it got here. We had it, so I am not worrying how it came.

I got a letter from Bud yesterday and one from Skip and Elizabeth and one from you and some from Jerry. Not bad for one day.

It's getting late in the fall now over here but you would never know it. It's still hot and it still rains.

You remember my old gal friend Helen Dillinger? Well Jerry wrote and told me she had a baby. It only lived for four days. Gee, Pappy, that was kind of tough. You know she was a pretty good kid.

I guess Dale and Elise are finally going to break their necks. Does it seem like two years in July since I got married? Somehow I can hardly believe it. I am thankful to you ever since for letting me get married. I have never been sorry, even though I am ten thousand miles away from her. I hope you never have reason to be sorry for letting me get married. Jerry has moved to Hershey. She hopes to move back to Hummelstown before I come home from the war.

Pappy, my outfit has been awarded the Bronze star for taking part in the campaign for New Guinea. So that is one decoration I can be proud of.

The Bronze Star is a United States decoration awarded to members of the United States Armed Forces for heroic achievement, heroic service, meritorious achievement, or meritorious service in a combat zone. It was first awarded February 4, 1944 (retroactive through December 7, 1941).

I saw General MacArthur[12]. I can't tell you where it was, but, anyway, I can now say I have seen him in person.

Pappy, I am glad you made me finish high school. There is some book work to do in this work here. The book-learning that I got at M.H.S. is coming in handy now. While this war is over I am going to school on government money and learn some more. The longer you are out of school the more you wish you would have studied harder.

I am really having a tough time catching up on my letter writing. I was out of stationery with the exception of this last sheet I got in a Christmas package from Rob Hoffman, a friend of Jerry's. So today I hopped it to the Red Cross Canteen and got some writing paper and envelopes. So I can make out for a few weeks. By that time, I should be able to get to the Red Cross again.

Pappy, I want to tell you while I am thinking about it. I am indebted to you for more things than I can ever hope to repay you for. The one thing I want to thank you for the most is for never letting me drink. Thanks to you I have never had a desire to drink. Some credit goes to Jerry, but most of it goes to you and for that I thank you.

Then, too, for Sunday School. Believe me, Pappy. If you pray to God for help you will get it. There is a lot of comfort in the Bible when you are feeling low.

Then, Pappy, you have also been a mother to me. For that I am grateful, too. So, Pappy, I just want to say Thanks for everything. I am proud I can call you Pappy.

I am in no danger, but I have just never told you before how thankful I am for such a father as you have been.

Tell Sis to keep her mouth shut. I can hear her clear over here in New Guinea. She kept me awake with her big mouth.

Keep your nose clean Pappy, and don't take any wooden quarters.

Good Luck and God Bless You, Pappy.

Bill

March 25, 1944
New Guinea

Hi, Pappy,

I got a package from Jerry today that she mailed November 23, so you see that sometimes it takes a little time to get here.

I have a picture of Billy now. He has Jerry's pug nose. It looks just like hers.

I got a letter from Eggie today. He says that he and Edith Harbold are right in the groove. He says that even Flash Miller got himself a steady girl, too. Things are moving right along on the home front.[13]

I got a roll of film today. When I get some snapshots taken I will send you one.

Boy, we had a storm one night last week that made any storm I ever saw look like a shower.

We had chicken today. We get some fresh meat now. But still get plenty of dried beef.

Boy, Pappy, I saw a native woman today and she looked pretty white.

How is Sis doing with her new teeth?

If you get another copy of my letter to Mr.

Johnston save it and give it to Jerry. I would like to read it when I get back home.

Gee, Pappy, I can't say much of anything else or the censor[14] will cut it out.

God Bless You, Your Son, Bill

March 29, 1944
New Guinea

Hi, Pappy,

Jerry has moved with her parents from 35 West Main to 343 West Main so I guess I will still be able to find her when I get back.

The censorship is starting to crank down a little more. So I'll just quit writing about things over on this side. Anyway, I can say we are still going strong.

It's raining now and looks like it will keep up all day. I got a letter from Aunt Bert last week. She said that Helen was turned down by the H.A.C. [Women's Army Corps, aka WAAC]

I hear that Dale Weaver is starting to get induction fever. I hope they put his ass in the infantry. He's been dodging the draft for two years now so I hope they give him the works.

Eggie must be doing O.K. at the Alexandria Air Base.[15] He says he likes it pretty good now.

Say "Hi" to all the guys that are left back home. Hoping to see them soon.

Good Luck, Bill

March 31, 1944
New Guinea

Hi, Pappy,

I got your letter today and so I will answer it while I have some time on my hands. I got a picture of Billy yesterday. He is sitting under the Christmas tree. He looks a little wild-eyed with excitement.

It's a dead as a grave around here now. I used to find more excitement around home. Tojo left this place in a hurry, so now we have no air raids or red alerts. It is as quiet as Middletown used to be after nine o'clock.

Eggie told me he is getting a lot of super reports and letters from Edith Harbold so I guess he must be on the G.I. ball.

You know, Pappy, I'm awfully proud of you, too. Where else can I find a guy like you? You have been a father, mother, and a good pa. To you I owe a lot. I'm glad now that you made me finish high school. Then, too, you never gave me seven kinds of hell when I made a mistake. You just showed me the mistakes and told me not to make them again. Then when I asked your permission to get married you just wanted to know if I loved Jerry and was it returned that she loved me. So I'm proud of you, Pappy, and am glad I am able to fight for you.

Well, nothing more to talk about so I'll write to you soon again.

Bill.

May 6, 1944
V-Mail, no place noted
Stamped by a censor

Hi Pappy,

I have missed again, Pappy. This time by boat. Now I have missed every way you can except to walk. I guess the next time I miss I will be old.[16]

We are encamped in a beautiful coconut grove. It is about 300 yards from the most beautiful beach I have ever seen. It runs along the ocean for miles lined with coconut trees. It still feels like the devil. Here there is a saying that we need not worry about Hell as we have spent a year there already.

But really, Pappy, don't worry because it is warm around here and I am unhurt so I am confident of the future. I even forget what a Jap plane looks like any more except the wrecked ones. They never come over any more. And yet we have no APO[17] here, so watch out for a new one when we ship.

May 9, 1944
New Guinea

Dear Pappy,

Last night I saw a show [movie] for a change. It was one I had seen last January, but I enjoyed it anyway. It seems that no matter how often you see a show over here you can still enjoy it. I think it's because for two hours you can forget New Guinea and the Japs. For two hrs. you are back in the grand U.S.A. Seeing real people was a slice of life that seems like your own. I thought I enjoyed shows back in the States, but I enjoy them twice as much over here.

Jerry sent me a watch. It's a Bulova. You remember the one you got me for graduation? I had broken it way down in Mobile one day while taking Commando Tactics. Jerry took it home with her when she came down to see me. Since I can't have it fixed until the damn war is over she sent me a new one. Anyway, it fell out of the box she sent it in at APO 321.[18] The Sgt. in charge of mail there put it back in the box and sent it to me. So I was indeed lucky to even get it.

One thing I must say about this Hell Hole is that they sure have beautiful moonlight nights. One thing the moon over here is really beautiful.

We have only had mail once since we got here. The prospects of getting any more is pretty poor. But anyway, when we do get it we should get a sack full.[19]

Anyhow we can write which helps out some. It is not half as bad waiting for mail as it is not being able to write and let you know I am O.K.

Sud said in his last letter that payday was about here and he was glad since he is badly broke. On the contrary, I don't care if they never pay us because we can't spend it. Anyway I was hoping to get a rest leave but things are popping over here now so I guess I will have to forget it for a while.

Say Hi to everyone for me. I am sending a shilling in this letter so tell me if you receive it.

Good Luck, Your Son, Bill

May 16, 1944
New Guinea

Dear Pappy,

Got your letter today. Can't say much because there is nothing to write about. Although it is winter it's so hot that all you do is sweat and you keep sweating until the sun goes down and, unless there is a breeze blowing, you sweat all night.

Since you sleep under a mosquito net it cuts the bugs down a lot. However, after midnight it gets cool and very damp. The dampness here is worse than it was in Mobile. Sometimes in the morning your blankets are so damp you can almost wring the water out of them.

Pappy, how bad is your rupture[20]? George told me in the letter I got from him today.

Yeah, Pappy, they are giving Germany the works. I hope we can really give Tojo the works

131

and I mean everything. I think something big is due to happen one of these fine days. I sure hope so. I have been in the jungle too long already. Nothing more to say.

I'm sorry to hear that Mr. Hoffman has passed away. I just got word from George today about him. In the same mail I got an Easter card from him and Mrs. Hoffman.[21]

I will write a long letter as soon as I can find time.

Good Luck, Your Son, Bill

May 21, 1944
New Guinea

Hi Pappy,

I have finally found someone here in New Guinea who I knew in civilian life. He is from Hummelstown and saw Billy when he was home in September. It's really swell to run across someone you knew back home.

His outfit has moved out but they are attached to the same service group we are so I should run across him again.

It's still hot here, Pappy. It has not rained for a while. I hope it rains all day one of these fine days because if it doesn't we will be living on a desert.

I have a year in the tropics now and my outfit should soon be getting a breakout. No kidding, it's really a wonder what a guy can take when he has to. Boy, if it wasn't for the medics though, it would be awful. I must say the medical corps is really on the ball.[22]

Mail here is piss-poor. We haven't had mail twice in four weeks.[23] Any day now we should get a truckload. Anyway, Bud should be getting back to the good old U.S.A. one of these fine months. I sure hope so. I guess he must have a little better than two years in now. Can't say much more here, Pappy.

Your Son, Bill

Long before invasion of the Philippines, the question had arisen among United States strategists as to what the next target would be. Originally the plan had been to bypass the Philippines and to conduct the B-29 strategic bombing program from bases in China. Subsequently, plans were made for the conquest of Taiwan as an additional base for B-29's after a foothold had been gained in the Philippines. However, with the overrunning of airfields and planned sites for B-29's by the Japanese in China, and with the Marianas available as a base for strategic bombing operations, a change of plans was indicated.

United States military strategists became embroiled in a behind-the-scenes debate as to what the next move should be. The outcome of this controversy was a decision on the part of the Joint Chiefs of Staff to make Luzon the next target, discard the plan to bomb Japan from bases in China, and bypass Taiwan.

From the Japanese perspective, control of the islands was vital. Loss of the Philippines would threaten Japan's overseas access to foodstuffs and critical raw materials, especially oil, from the East Indies and Southeast Asia. Thus, Tokyo's naval and army leaders had vowed to make the defense of the Philippines their major war effort for 1943-44.

For these purposes, General Tomoyuki Yamashita, the former conqueror of British Malaya and Singapore and the commander of Japanese land forces in the Philippines, had some 430,000 troops stationed all across the islands, while Japanese naval leaders were prepared to commit the entire battle fleet to this mission. If the Americans could be stopped here, then perhaps the entire tide of the war could be changed or, at least, Japan's position greatly strengthened.

During the spring of 1944, the Joint Chiefs had debated the merits of seizing Luzon or the Chinese island of Formosa as an initial point for direct operations against Japan. Admiral Ernest J. King, the Chief of Naval Operations, had long objected to landings in the Philippines, and by May 1944 he was joined by Army Chief of Staff General George C. Marshall and Army Air Force Chief of Staff General Henry H. Arnold.

Marshall felt that it made more sense to "cut across" from the Mariana Islands to Formosa. MacArthur, on the other hand, argued that the Formosa route was militarily "unsound" and that the Philippine Islands provided a more sensible staging area for the final assault against the Japanese home islands.

General Douglas MacArthur, commander of the Philippine defenses in 1941, felt a strong moral responsibility to free the entire archipelago of the brutal Japanese occupation. He had also made a very vocal pronouncement that he would return and free the Philippines, thus giving his Southwest Pacific command a key mission (and perhaps honor and glory to his already stellar career).

On the other hand, the enlisted men had little knowledge of these plans and were living in a rather calm day-to-day way of life.

May 25, 1944
New Guinea

Dear Pappy,

I am sending a bracelet along in your letter for Barbara Ann. I don't want to send two in Helen's letter so please give it to Barbara Ann.

Gee, Pappy, no mail for two weeks. I sure could stand a few letters for a change. I suppose when I do get mail I will have so much that it will take a month to answer it all. But I won't mind at all!

I get a chance to go swimming every day so now I am getting my tan back that I lost when I moved from 503 to 322.

Please send me a pipe and some socks and a knife if you have one. It you don't, however, don't worry. The army here issued one that fulfills all requirements. However, I think in one of Mary's letters she told me you had one to send. All you needed was my written request.

I have enough bracelets for the others; however, in the process of getting moved, I lost one. In other words, I don't have enough to go around and I am going to send it to Peggy. Jerry and her mother and Sis already have theirs so if they ask any questions you can tell them.

Hoping the war is soon over.   Your son, Bill

May 27, 1944
New Guinea

It's hot as the devil and already it's only ten o'clock. I am on guard so I am trying to catch up a little bit on letter writing.

In one of your letters you said something about a father with several children being drafted. You think that fathers should not be drafted. I can't see that way. Half the guys in my outfit have children. We have about ten or twelve guys who have never even seen their children. You probably think well, they knew they were going to get in the war. So what? Don't we all have the right to have a wife and family whether there is a war or not? Our C.O. enlisted and he has a wife and child.

About half the men in the Company have children. I don't mean just one. I mean two, three, or four children. Won't the Government have to keep them all? From December 7, 1941 to January 1, 1944 there were 139,850 men killed, wounded or missing in the armed forces. During that same period there were 18,500[24] killed at home. You said the Government will have to take care of the dependents of soldiers who died. How many of them had dependents? Who is going to take care of the dependents of these 18,500 who were killed in civilian life if the Government doesn't?

I say draft them all before you draft the women. If half the guys in the army are married and almost that many have children, why should they leave the rest of them at home? Doesn't a married man have as much to fight for as a single man? I say he has more.

We still don't get much mail. So I can't answer any questions you may have asked me. Please tell me if you get the bracelet O.K.

Your Son, Bill

Reconquest of the Philippines

In the Philippines the principal objective had been Luzon since it was on one of the corners of the so-called strategic triangle. Since it was presumed that the Japanese had massed their principal ground, air, and naval strength in Luzon, United States strategists had planned to gain a foothold first in southernmost Mindanao, then move to Leyte, and finally to Luzon after air supremacy had been gained over that area.

By July 1944 most of the military planners agreed that an invasion of Formosa was not logistically feasible in the near future. In September the Joint Chiefs thus approved a December starting date for MacArthur's invasion of Leyte

Island, its first objective in the central Philippines. (The invasion was to be followed by an assault on either Luzon, the large, northernmost Philippine island, on February 20 or Formosa on March 1, 1945.) But it was not until October (1944) that Admiral King finally agreed that Luzon was the better choice.

However, when naval reconnaissance in September 1944 revealed little Japanese activity in the Philippines, Admiral Halsey proposed landing directly on Leyte in October. This change of strategy was quickly approved by the U.S. Chiefs of Staff, who were at that time attending the second Quebec Conference. Strategically the plan was brilliant, because it would force the Japanese to split their forces in the Philippines and practically force the Japanese Combined Fleet to come out in the open to meet the threat.

The amphibious assault on Leyte took place on October 20, 1944 with four divisions of the U.S. Sixth Army going in abreast. The invading force included the XXIV Corps from the Central Pacific. Initial opposition was light, but the Japanese, who had expected to make their main stand on Luzon, decided to shift their remaining air and naval forces against the U.S. military in Leyte. They were also successful for a time in sending large numbers of ground reinforcements to Leyte, and the Sixth Army found itself engaged in a major struggle.

As had been anticipated, the attack on Leyte presented the Japanese Navy with a challenge it could not ignore. Gathering together its remaining strength, the Japanese Combined Fleet converged on Leyte Gulf in three columns, and for a time this seriously threatened the success of the whole Leyte operation. (Actually, the sea battle was a series of engagements lasting from October 23 to the 26th.) In the end, Japan's fleet was almost completely destroyed, and for the rest of the war Allied naval forces were in virtual control of the surface of the Pacific.

Two months of heavy ground fighting took place in Leyte before American troops had secured parts of the island necessary for air and logistical bases, before the Army Air Forces had gained air superiority, and before naval and air forces had stopped Japanese reinforcing operations. Late in December General MacArthur announced that thereafter the U.S. Eighth Army would assume combat responsibility for the Leyte-Samar area.

July 18, 1944
APO 920 [25]

—Bill's unit has moved again.

Hi Pappy,

I am soon getting a rest leave, pretty soon I hope. If I get it I will really be glad to get out of here for a little while. It is for two days plus traveling time.

I know it's a long time between letters, but it can't be helped. I'm sorry it's that way. I hope it will improve as time goes by. It really keeps me busy writing to Jerry these days.

It's still hot here. Even though it's winter

now you can't tell it except that it is starting to rain a lot. I'm sorry, Pappy, I can't send anything back from here. After a while I should, but right now I can only say nothing doing.

One thing, I have been able to go to church. I can go only every other Sunday, but believe me, it's wonderful to be able to go to church again.

I hope that in another two weeks I can write and tell you a little bit about Australia. I don't see many natives here. I am glad. Most of them only want your cigarettes and Australian money. Boy, is that invasion going O.K. The Russians are really going to town.

Pappy, I sure hope the war is over soon. I am really sweating it. I am about tired of this war. Anyway, Pappy, I am making out A.O.K. So I say Good Luck!

Your Son, Bill

August 9, 1944
South West Pacific – APO 920

Hi, Pappy,

Jerry told me you have not heard from me for a while. I am sorry but I have been writing to you. If you have not heard yet, I am sorry, but I am sure you should have heard.

I am still sweating out my rest leave. But as yet, nothing doing.

I sent Jerry some pictures of the natives. If you pay to get a set made from them I'll tell Jerry to get them made for you. Write and tell her that you want a set.

I am on K.P. tomorrow which means a rough day ahead.

I heard from Pud last week. I also heard from Eggie, but as yet I have had no time to answer.

We still have a few air raids but outside of that it's pretty quiet.

I see where they are doing OK over in Europe. They have a real all-American team over there. It looks like they can't be stopped anymore. Hope the war is over,

God Bless You, Bill

August 17, 1944
SWPA
APO 920

Hi, Pappy,

I hit the jackpot today at mail call. Heard from you, George, and Jerry.

I am writing in the mess hall. We use the mess hall because it serves the double purpose of mess and day room.

You are right about raising hell with the Germans, and the Nips are sweating, too. I mean they are getting the works.

It rains a lot. In fact, it has rained all day and looks like it will rain all night.

I don't think I will be going on a furlough for a while, but I still have hope.

Boy, the St. Louis Cards are really out in front in the National League. It may be a nickel[26] world series. That is, if the Browns don't fold up. I hope I can listen to them over the radio.

Pappy, I wish you could see the swell roads we have here now. It's not long since we took the place but the engineers have really built some swell roads.[27]

Say hello to everyone for me. Tell them I am still kicking. In fact, tell them I am OK except that I have "statesick" which means I am wanting to get back to the good old United States.

Don't let anyone give you any lead quarters.

Your Son, Bill

August 20, 1944
SWPA

Hi, Pappy,

It looks like Adolph will soon throw in the towel. Ivd and the boys are really giving them the works. I think perhaps old Tojo did a wise thing when he quit the Nip government. It looks like we are sort of getting even for Pearl Harbor, doesn't it?[28]

I am on guard and since I have a candle with me I am writing letters.

Here where I am on guard they don't have electric lights. However, back at my own camp we have a light in each tent.

Don't have to worry much about air raids right now since there is no moon. But still I stick sort of close to my foxhole.[29]

I wish you could see my foxhole[30], Pappy. It's a thing of beauty. It's about ten feet long and three feet deep. Since the coral here is like rock, we did not go down so deep. We get some sand bags and build it up. For the roof we have logs and some scrap tin. One time on this we piled sandbags. It holds five or so, whichever the case calls for. It's about 5 ft. from the farthest bunk and right along mine and another guy's. Believe me, when we have a red alert we really get in there on the double quick.

There are five guys in my tent including myself. So the old foxhole is the best place in camp. I remember one time when I was caught in an air raid out partially by the bay. I was alone in a foxhole. It was a swell foxhole. But with no one else there to sweat it out with you, a foxhole is the most lonesome place in the world. I hope I never have to sweat out an air raid alone again.

Last week I talked to a sailor who had just come over from the States. He said the women are still beautiful, so I guess things are still OK back in the good ole U.S.A. As long as women have time to make themselves beautiful things are not yet desperate.

Pap, it looks like it may be a nickel world series between the Cards and the Browns.

Boy, am I going to miss the football games this year. Last year I was a rookie, still scared at the noise of the jungle and did not take notice of football and so on. This year I know the score and so I find time to see how things look in the sports world.

Tell Sis to watch her waistline as she used to eat too much when I was home. Helen tells me she lost weight while she was working. However, she hopes to gain it back.

Good Luck, Your Son, Bill

August 31, 1944
South West Pacific

Hi, Pappy,

In yesterday's letter Jerry told me she likes coming over home for a week. So I guess you will have your hands full with the three youngsters there.[31]

I got a letter from Pud yesterday. He said to tell you he is still O.K.[32]

Have not heard from Eggie for quite a while but I guess he is busy these days with Jim Slough.

I saw pictures of the invasion; it must have been pretty awful for both sides.

Things are getting too civilized around here. Nude swimming is no longer allowed because there are females in the area. I hope we move. Women spoil a place. No kidding, women are fine and beautiful but this is no place for them. I really hope we move out now but quick. I think before long we will have to wear shirts. Wearing a shirt is fine back home where it is civilized. But over here where there is a war being fought, I can't see it.

All things of civilization are fine. But over here you get used to living with only things that are necessary. No one who was raised in civilization forgets in two years all his bringing up. But while you are over here, I think they should make allowances.

Anyway, Pappy, I guess I have done enough growling for a while.

We have a swell gang of men in this outfit. We have a job and we are doing it. We are proud and I think we have a right to be. Nor are we forgetting that if it was not for you people giving up the stuff to do it with, we could not do it. Thanks to people like yourself and all the American people we can now see victory ahead of us. Thanks Pap to you and everyone back there I will soon be back in God's land with all my loved ones.

Your Son, Bill

September 15, 1944
S. W. P.

Hi, Pappy,

I received your letter yesterday so I shall try to answer it today.

I was on KP yesterday so I am off all day today. I washed clothes and cleaned my equipment this morning so now I am catching up on letter writing.

I heard from Eggie last week, and from John Rider, too.

Pud should make it home when the war in Europe is over. He has been over there a long time now, so he should be one of the first back.

It's really getting hot over here now, and summer is just around the corner.

At the Front 1942–1945

[It is presumable here that Bill had heard from Pud and knew that he had been part of what ultimately would be three major invasions in the European Theatre of WW II. As a result Bill was expressing that Pud was overdue to be one of the first to be sent home to the States. Pud had already served in two of the three major invasions in the European Theatre—the first as part of the North Africa Invasion (likely in Operation Torch in November 1942) and the second, the Normandy Invasion (D-Day) in June 1944. At the date of this writing he would soon be facing the third, the Battle of the Bulge, that began in December 1944 and where ultimately there would be 89,500 American casualties.]

I thought the Browns would take the pennant, but they have slid into third place. By the time you get this letter the World Series will be started, I guess.

It's quiet around here now except for air raids and now they are growing scarce.

We are getting to see some late shows and we have made an ice box out of lumber and sawdust. We use a half horse power motor for the current so now we have ice water most of the time.

The snow will soon be flying by, Pappy. It's two years since I have seen snow. Boy, would I like to do some ice skating this year. Next year I hope I will be back where I can see snow and ice instead of just reading about it.

I guess that's about all I can think of for this time.

Your son, Bill

MacArthur's return to the Philippines began on the island of Leyte in October 1944. (Prior to the amphibious assault, the Japanese carrier force had been decimated in the battle of the Philippine Sea on June 19-20 of the same year.) Moreover, the Battle of Leyte Gulf in October saw most of the Japanese surface fleet destroyed with little to show for its sacrifice. Japan's once formidable air force was also decimated, leaving the skies over the Philippines open to American air power.

The primary objective of assaulting Leyte itself was to provide a staging area for a much larger effort, the assault against the island of Luzon where most of the Japanese land defenses lay. Before U.S. forces could launch the attack on Luzon, however, a base of operation needed to be established close to the island. Airbases had to be established in order to provide the advancing troops with air support. It is believed that Pfc. William H. Calhoon was part of the building of the airstrip and preparing the surrounding areas.

October 12, 1944
Netherlands East Island

Hi, Pappy,

I am still OK and kicking. Still hot as the devil over here.

Saw a swell show last night. "Song of the Open Road."

Boy, the Cards came through to take the series. The Browns really lost some dough by their move.

We are busy, I mean BUSY, all the time. But since we are getting the war over with I am not kicking.

It has not rained for several days, so I guess we will get a real storm before long.

So Don Miller is out of the army. He must have been in worse shape than I thought he was. Well, if he can't take the army life back there he sure could not take it over here. The Field Artillery really has a rough go of it over here.

Cal is really seeing action. I guess Cherbourg and Normandy is as close a place [meaning as close to the action] as you can get into it.

I don't believe Bud will make it home until the war in Europe is over. As for me, I can't say how much longer I will be over here. Perhaps when the war is over in Europe, rotation will get to be a thing of reality instead of a dream.

Football is in full swing again. Notre Dame really put the works to Pitt. According to the paper over here, Notre Dame is the best in the nation again. I would like to see Georgia Tech *play. I believe Notre Dame can beat them. If Middletown beats Hummelstown I am really going to raze Jerry.*

Boy, would I like to do some rabbit and squirrel hunting this year.

Lights out, time to get in bed.

Your Son, Bill

Meanwhile, American and Australian forces invaded the Philippines on October 20 and between October 23 and 26, the Battle of Leyte Gulf, as it became known, was fought in the waters of that gulf near the Philippine Islands of Leyte, Samar, and Luzon. This was part of a strategy aimed at isolating Japan from the countries it had occupied in Southeast Asia and, in particular, depriving Japan's forces and industries of vital oil supplies.

The Imperial Japanese Navy (IJN) mobilized nearly all of its remaining major naval vessels in an attempt to defeat the Allied invasion in four separate engagements: the the Battle of the Sibuyan Sea, the Battle of Surigao Strait, the Battle of Cape Engaño, and the Battle off Samar, as well as other actions.

By the time of the actual battles, Japan had fewer aircraft than the Allied forces had sea vessels, demonstrating the difference in power of the two sides at this point of the war. Repulsed by the U.S. Navy's 3rd and 7th Fleets, the IJN failed to achieve its objective, suffered very heavy losses, and never sailed to battle in comparable force thereafter. Further, the majority of Japan's surviving heavy ships, deprived of fuel, remained in their bases for the rest of the Pacific War. Notably, this is the first battle in which Japanese aircraft carried out organized kamikaze attacks.

Importantly, the Battle of Leyte Gulf is generally considered to be the largest naval battle of World War II and very possibly, the largest naval battle in history.

On October 20, 1944, a few hours after his troops had first landed, but before a shot was fired, General MacArthur had waded ashore onto the Philippine island of Leyte. Later that day, he made a radio broadcast in which he declared, "People of the Philippines, I have returned!"

The following is a letter written by a Navy enlistee who had participated in the Leyte Island Invasion. Written November 8, 1944 and postmarked November 12 with the return address of San Francisco and stamped with *"Passed By Naval Censor,"* Johnny Wayne had written across the top margin of his letter to his Aunt Jessie Pifer, *"P.S., I don't think it wise to tell Mother of these battles. She'll only worry."*

At Sea, November 8, 1944

Dear Aunt Jeb,

How is everything going with you? I'm a little dehydrated myself. I suppose you have heard of the wonder of science – dehydrated food. Curse the man that started that. Because of him I weigh 20 pounds less. Now the Navy is letting up on writing a little this time. You've probably read about the "I-have-returned-to-the-Philippines"-man, MacArthur. I wish he were the only man here.

So you know, I took part in the Leyte Island invasion. Also the big Naval engagement that followed. The Naval battles took place in the Surigao Strait between Leyte Gulf and the Sulu Sea. I don't believe I've ever seen a Fourth of July any more beautiful. It took place in the early morning. Still dark. When the ships started firing at each other the guns left long white arches to their targets. It seems the whole sky was covered with lines like your July 4th sky rockets.

The only thing I didn't like was the Japs were firing back at us with guns, just as big. One Naval Battle that big is enough to last a man a lifetime. I'm glad it was the Japs that were swimming after the battle and not me. After it's all over maybe I can tell you more about the Island and one of these days we'll stroll down the street in PA. Three pages is the limit, Jeb.

Love, John A. Wayne S'16 [32]

His Aunt Jessie likely rejoiced at this good news, full of hope that with this victory over the Japanese Johnny might not see any worse action. But Okinawa was yet to come.

November 30, 1944
Philippine Islands — APO 72 [33]

Hi, Cappy,

Still very busy here in the Philippines. I burned my hand last week so I could not write.

I had a letter from Jerry today with my new APO on it, so I guess by this time you should have my first letter.

Heard from Pud last week. He said to tell you his outfit is moving around a lot, but that he was O.K. Heard from Clam [Clarence]. In fact, I heard from you and from everyone but Cappy.

It's pretty hot here. But we are slowly putting the clips to Tojo. Whenever I think how far I

have come since I left the States it really builds up my morale. I think we have come over halfway in the defeat of Japan. Perhaps 1945 will tell the story. I don't believe I will come home for several months yet. But I just hope the year 1945 is as successful and goes just as fast.

I was in the kitchen for about a week, but you don't get food that can be cooked, so after I caught the devil from our mess sergeant I told him to stick the kitchen, so I am out on line duty again.

Jerry's cousin Paul Martin went back from over here and has asked for service in the Pacific again. He was in Pearl Harbor so I guess he wants to go along to Tokyo.

I see where the boys in Europe have finally got going again. That makes me feel better, too.

Today is Thanksgiving and I have several good reasons to be thankful. First off, I am thankful I am still alive and kicking; next to being in the Philippines, then thankful for you and all the good friends back home and that I am one year being closer home than I was last year. We did not have turkey but we had fresh hamburger which beats C-rations by a mile.

Anyhow, Pappy, I can still say I am able to laugh and enjoy life pretty good, so I am sure I will make out O.K.

I guess we will soon have shows here. As yet there are just a few too many air raids to risk it.

I have time to go to church now which is a big help. We have the same chaplain we had about 14 months ago down at APO 503. We were assigned to another group for a while. He is from some place in Pennsylvania.

We are getting the camp area cleaned up now. We have showers and lights which are a great help.

I think we will get a lot of stateside chow instead of chow from Australia. I don't care much for Australian chow. We have had fresh butter about four times since we were here. I am sure that if we are lucky enough to stay where we are now until Christmas we will have turkey with all the trimmings with fresh spuds.

Don't take any wooden dimes.

God Bless You, Your Son, Bill

December 20, 1944
Philippines Island
APO 72 (Leyte)

Dear Pappy,

We have not had any regular mail for two weeks and so I can hardly wait. The funny part of it is that we have been getting packages.

Things look tough over in Germany again. The Germans are tearing up their own place so when we finally beat them they should remember the lessons for a long time.

Sometimes it's hard to believe that I have been away for two years and I think perhaps in another two I will be home. I hope so anyway.

Some guys I took basic training with just came back up from Australia where they went the same time I reached Guinea. They have been down there all this time.

The last time I heard from Pud he was still O.K. He said that it gets cold over there (referring to Europe), really cold.

It does not rain so much anymore and at least you can walk around camp without getting covered with mud.

We have most of our washing done by the Filipinos and that helps a lot.

We have a screen in the company now and so we have shows which are a big help to make the time go by.

I hear that Bing Crosby is on his way over here. I hope so because he is without doubt the best singer in the States.

We get a lot of magazines from special services and even if they are two or three months old they make for good reading.

I hope I can hear some bowl games on the day after New Year's. Remember we are one day ahead of you back in the States.

I am expecting to take a razzing from Jerry whenever I get mail from her. I think perhaps H.H.S beat M.H.S. this year and so the raspberries from her.

The Nips don't come around much anymore and so my morale is good. Here's hoping to see you in '45.

Your Son, Bill

The operations on Leyte gave the Americans little more than a foothold in the Philippines. Then in December, troops under Brigadier General William C. Dunckel, captured the island of Mindoro, with the assistance of the 7th fleet.

With the capture of Mindoro, U.S. forces were positioned south of Luzon. However, MacArthur intended to land his forces at Lingayen, farther north, which would place his troops close to several roads and railways on Luzon, which lead to Manila (the capital city and the main objective) through the plains in the center of the island.

A strategic decision was made for U.S. aircraft to make reconnaissance and bombing flights over southern Luzon, intending to deceive the Japanese forces into believing that the attack on Luzon would come from the south. Further, transport aircraft were used to make parachute drops with dummies. In addition, minesweepers were used to clear the bays of Balayan, Batanbas, and Tayabas, located to the south of Luzon where Filipino resistance fighters conducted sabotage operation in southern Luzon.

However, General Yamashita, leader of the Imperial Japanese Army in the Philippines, was not convinced by the deception and built significant defensive positions in the hills and mountains surrounding the Lingayen Gulf in Northern Luzon. By December 28 two airbases were controlled by the U.S. and were ready to assist in the attack on Luzon, scheduled for January 1945.

December 31, 1944
Philippine Islands

Dear Dad,

We had turkey for Christmas and we are having it tomorrow night again. Boy, what chow for a change.

I had a bad ear and have been confined to quarters for a week now. But one or two more days and it will be O.K.

Pud sure has a nice rifle from what I can tell from the picture you sent. I always thought it one of the best I ever saw.

As for Notre Dame, what a lacing they took this year. I never heard the like before, no kidding. As for the Browns, I did not pick them. In fact, I won about 30 pence [$15] on them.

Now I am sweating out the Rose Bowl. I have picked Southern California.[34]

According to the news tonight they have checked the Germans and have pushed them back in some spots. Boy, am I glad to hear that.

Pap, Jerry told me you are taking it kind of hard since Eggy is in the infantry. Please, Dad, believe me that he will be O.K. It's a tougher life than the Air Corps but they will make sure he is well-trained and ready if he comes over. I have worked with them under fire and they can take care of themselves. I think you will find Eggy won't like it too well, but I'm sure everything will be O.K.

Roosevelt sure is the guy for me. But I did not think he would carry Pennsylvania the way he did. He sure is giving us soldiers all the breaks he can. Glad to see him again as my Commander-in-Chief.

Love, Your Son, Bill

World War II: 1945

MacArthur's Landing in bronze by Anastacio Caedo commemorates the historic landing of General Douglas MacArthur in the Leyte Gulf at the start of the campaign to recapture and liberate the Philippines from Japanese occupation on October 20, 1944. Regrettably, only one-third of the men MacArthur had left behind on March 11, 1942, when he had announced "I shall return," survived to see this fulfilled promise.

Transportation of troops during wars is always a major endeavor. World War II presented its own challenges as the United States was initially ill-prepared and was faced with moving millions of men (and women) to two huge areas of the world, simply identified as the European Theatre and the Pacific Theatre. As the US did not have ships to do the transport, they looked to mass-producing what were known generally as "cargo ships" to meet the maritime transport needs.

In early 1941, the US Maritime Commission placed an order for 260 ships of the Liberty design. Of these, 60 were for

Britain. Over the next four years, US shipyards would produce 2,751 Liberty Ships. The majority (1,552) of these came from new yards built on the West Coast and operated by Henry J. Kaiser. Best known for building the Bay Bridge and the Hoover Dam, Kaiser pioneered new shipbuilding techniques.

Components were built all across the US and transported to shipyards where the vessels could be assembled in record time. During the war, a Liberty Ship could be built in about two weeks at a Kaiser yard. By 1943, three Liberty Ships were being completed each day.

Initially these mass-produced ships had a poor public image because of their questionable construction (riveted together) by assembly line. In a speech announcing the emergency shipbuilding program at the beginning of the war, the President, with a mixture of humor and deadly seriousness, referred to the ship as a "dreadful looking object." Nonetheless, on September 27, 1941 an announcement was made that the ships were being constructed and the first vessel was launched with Roosevelt remarking that the new class of ships would "bring liberty to Europe," which led to the name this cargo carrier the "Liberty" ship.

In September 1943 strategic plans and shortage of more suitable transport required that Liberty ships be pressed into emergency use as troop transports with about 225 vessels eventually converted for this purpose. Some in the Southwest Pacific were turned into makeshift troop transports for New Guinea operations. Beginning in April 1944 these Liberty ships provided mobile depot support for B-29 bombers based on Guam, Iwo Jima, and Okinawa. As it turned out, they were essential to the war effort.

The Final Thrust on Luzon

Capture of the Marianas had brought the island of Japan to within reach of the Army Air Forces' huge new bomber, the B-29, a plane that was able to make a nonstop flight of the 1,400 miles from this small island in the Philippines to Tokyo and back. Construction of airfields to accommodate B-29s had begun in the Marianas even before the shooting had stopped, and in late November 1944 the strategic bombing of Japan began.

From all indications, although for military security reasons not specifically stated in his letters he wrote home, Bill Calhoon was part of the large contingent of various Special Forces who would have been instrumental in the major construction of these airfields needed for the B-29's.

The destruction to be dealt to Japan cities by these B-29s would be enormous. Much of Japan's industrial force was still intact in early 1945, but was idled by the serious shortage of raw materials which the Allied naval blockade had caused. Although thousands of Japanese civilians were killed and literally millions were made homeless by this air bombing, only a relatively small percentage of Japan's industrial facilities were destroyed, not enough to seriously affect the Japanese capacity to resist the attack they were under in late 1944.

Admiral William Halsey held the responsibility for the naval forces in the Philippine Sea—particularly in the Leyte Gulf engagement, and, as such, was charged with conducting these air raids against Japanese airfields, which he did admirably.

In mid-December 1944, after Halsey had led this successful campaign against the Japanese, his fleet was attempting to refuel its ships, especially the lighter destroyers, which had small fuel tanks. However, as the weather worsened it became increasingly difficult to refuel, and the attempts to do so had to be discontinued.

Despite warning signs of worsening conditions and the possibility of a typhoon, Halsey ordered that the ships remain at their stations while he kept tuned on short-wave radio to the limited information that was available, alert to any warning of possible danger before deciding what course of action to take. Finally the word came; his fleet would not be in the path of the typhoon.

Regrettably, this information given to Halsey about the location and direction of the typhoon was inaccurate; however, he had no way to know that the information he received was completely wrong.

Thus, rather than moving away from the area, on December 17, Halsey unwittingly sailed his Third Fleet directly into the heart of the typhoon. Because of 100 mph winds, very high seas and torrential rain, three destroyers capsized and sank, and 790 lives were lost. Nine other warships were damaged, and over 100 aircraft were wrecked or washed overboard. (Bill found out later that his brother Clarence "Clam" was serving aboard one of the vessels in the fleet, but he was not one of the casualties.)

On January 9, 1945, the assault on Luzon began. The Japanese forces were the first to report that more than 70 Allied warships were entering the Lingayen Gulf, where they began with pre-assault bombardments of Japanese shore positions, followed by shore landings of troops who faced strong opposition from Japanese kamikaze aircraft.

In keeping with the overall strategic military plan agreed upon by the leadership, the U.S. Sixth Army made a massive amphibious assault on Luzon along the shores of the Lingayen Gulf. The Japanese commander, General Tomoyuki Yamashita, had not intended to defend the Central Plains-Manila Bay area, but wanted only to pin down major elements of MacArthur's forces in order to delay Allied progress toward defeat of Japan.

However, strong Japanese forces—primarily their navy—chose to disregard Yamashita's plan and held out in Manila while Yamashita concentrated his forces in three mountainous strongholds where they could conduct an extended defense. This was a mistake, because a powerful American force then drove down the central valley from the Gulf of Manila.

A second amphibious landing took place on January 15 southwest of Manila when approximately 175,000 U.S. troops landed along the beachhead within a few days with other military corps protecting their flanks; they advanced south toward Manila. The U. S. forces did not meet much resistance until January 23 when they reached Clark Air Base and were stalled. There on January 31 two regiments of the U.S. 11th Airborne made an assault, capturing a bridge, later advancing toward Manila.

Bill Calhoon's first letter to his father in 1945 was written two weeks after Christmas 1944, after the November bombings had started, but before the full assault on Luzon had begun. The contrast between the major battles being fought and the letters being written home is an interesting study in the reality of war.

Philippine Islands
January 6, 1945

Dear Daddy,

Today I hit the jackpot in mail call with a letter from you, Helen, the young people from church, and four from Jerry. One of Jerry's was written on Christmas Day.

The last week we have been getting real honest chow, fresh meat about every other day, and pie most of the time.

I feel pretty good about the election. Once more Roosevelt was elected to be my Commander-in-Chief and I am proud to serve under him.

Too bad about Don Miller. Someone told me he took getting a Medical Discharge pretty tough. Maybe after a while he will get over that feeling and make a go of it.[1]

Pud should be getting a break[2] if things go OK over there. As for me, I am hoping, but so far there is nothing to indicate anything happening.

I got a V-Mail Christmas greeting from Pud, and Jerry had told me he was moving. I haven't heard from Clam or Eggy for a while.

Love, Your Son, Bill

Not hearing from Clam could be forgiven since, as noted above, at this time he was part of the Naval attacks in the Luzon offensive, so would not have been writing letters that would have arrived prior to Bill's January 6 letter to Pap saying he had not heard from Clam.

Philippine Islands
APO 72[3]
January 20, 1945

Hi, Pappy,

From what Clam told me in his letter today[4] he thinks he is coming out my way on his next trip. It seems like a lot of guys are coming this way.[5]

We have a radio station here in the Philippines. One thing I must give Madam Tojo is that she has it over our radio for music. No kidding, Pappy, Radio Tokyo really puts out some music. As you know, she tries to break our morale down with propaganda, but we just listen to her music.[6] Then we laugh at her when she starts shooting the bull.

No kidding, Pappy, things are going swell over here. Since I came to the Philippines it seems that at last we are no longer beating our heads against a stone wall. Down in Guinea it seemed as if we would never get out of the jungle. Now

169

we can see that we are getting somewhere.

We still don't get many of our packages yet, but your letters come through pretty good.

There is an acute shortage of soap and cigarettes but it should be over in a few weeks. Our chow still continues to be good, although it seems strange that it should be good for such a long time.

I hope '45 brings victory and I hope Bud soon gets back.

Your son, Bill

Philippine Islands
APO 321[7]
January 28, 1945

Hi, Pappy,

Once more we have a new camp. We came by plane this time.

We took off just at daybreak. The sun really looks beautiful from above the clouds. It was cold when we took off, but by the time we got here it was hot in the cabin of the plane. It was a longer ride than any of the others and I really enjoyed it.

You just can't describe the thrill of being in the air. If I ever get a chance, I would like to fly the whole way to the States by plane.

This place is tops. Hot in the day and cold at night. In many other ways it reminds me of Indiantown Gap.

We had corn on the cob last night and it tasted super.

I am a baker's helper right now. I help the bakers make pies and cakes. I don't think it will last long but I like it.

I hope the war ends in '45.

Love, Your Son, Bill

Philippine Islands
February 2, 1945

Hi, Sis and Pappy,

Boy, it's swell in this part of the Philippines. We are not as far north as we intend to go,⁵ but I have good hopes of getting there.

We are out by ourselves, so we have a chance to get fresh vegetables from the Filipinos. We have had roasting ears three times since we have been here.

I am now undergoing a kind of lesson in helping the bakers at night. They are teaching me to bake. That is, if they can.

We bake about 400 biscuits a night. The night before last we baked cherry pies. I made the filling and, believe it or not, they liked it. We have to bake over 500 biscuits tonight so I will soon have to go to work.

We have a good radio now and we really have some swell programs from back in the states. We have, that is, the army has, a radio station here in the Philippines and we get the programs from there. The night before last we had a Command Performance.[9] I heard Shirley Temple, Fibber McGee and Molly, Ginny Simms, and Dinah Shore all in the same program. Every night we have Fred Waring. No advertisements, either.

I like this place a whole lot, Pappy. The way the war is going suits me fine, too! We are going to town over here and in Germany, too. I don't think the Germans can stop us this time. As for the Nips, we are going to surprise them a lot more, too. Believe me, Pappy, we are going to really put the clips to the Nips![10]

Tell Helen I will write soon. I don't think I will have time tonight. I want to write Jerry a letter before we start to bake.

Your Son, Bill

Manila

On February 3 the 1ˢᵗ Cavalry Division captured the bridge across Tullahan River leading to the city of Manila; they advanced into the city that evening and the battle for the capture of Manila began.

On February 4 the paratroopers of the 11th Airborne—approaching the city from the south—arrived first to the main Japanese defenses south of the city of Manila where their advance was halted by heavy resistance. General Yamashita had ordered his troops to destroy all bridges and other vital installations as soon as the U.S. forces entered the city and, as ordered, Japanese forces, entrenched throughout the city, continued to resist U.S. Forces.

On the same day (February 4) General MacArthur announced that the recapture of Manila was imminent. Then on February 11, the 11th Airborne Division captured the last Japanese outer defenses, thus encircling the whole capital city. U.S. and Filipino forces carried out clearing operations in Manila in the following weeks. Military casualties totaled 1,010 Americans, 3,079 Filipinos, and 12,000 Japanese.

Next was the Battle for the Recapture of Corregidor, February 16-26, 1945, where American forces were pitted against the defending Japanese garrison on the island fortress. Because General MacArthur was obsessively committed to make up for the surrender of Corregidor to the Japanese in 1942, he showed no hesitation in designating the bulk of US and Philippine forces under his command. Others agreed with his view of Corregidor as an important symbol in United States history—the last Pacific outpost of any size that had fallen to

the enemy in the early stages of the Pacific War. The tables now
were turned against the Japanese.

The Philippines Islands
APO 321
February 16, 1945

Hi, Pappy,

From the news I would say the Russians are
still putting the clips to the Nazis. We are going
pretty good with the Nips. Believe me, Pap, the
yellow bastards are going to pay for burning Manila
and for each Yank and Filipino they have killed.
Listen to the news. Things are going to blow wide
open one of these days.

Boy, I don't think Jerry will ever let me forget
about the Hummelstown-Middletown game. She does
not say much in her letters, but I don't think it
will be that way when I get home.

Jerry told me Cal and Glen are back over my way
now. I might run across them up north some time.

I like my job of helping the bakers. I can bake
cakes and biscuits. Somehow I am learning to
make pies, too. But it's not as easy as cake.

Still quiet around here so now we have a ball
team. Lost 2 and won 3 so far. Every outfit has a

diamond here. No kidding, Pappy, we really have some beautiful diamonds here. We won our game tonight 9-7. I had 2 hits for 3 tries. The last time I was up we had two men on bases, two out, and I struck out. I mean _I struck out on the last strike._ I felt like bawling, I was so mad.

We are going strong, Pappy; it's rough, tough going, but we will beat them. You can bet on that.

We still have not received any Christmas packages.

Thanks for the swell Valentine. It came in mail call today.

I have pretty high hopes that this war will soon be over. I mean I am tired of it. I can't say when, but, boy, it sure looks good."

God Bless You and Keep You,

Your Son, Bill

Philippine Islands
APO 321
February 21, 1945

Hi, Daddy,

Jerry tells me you are having a nice winter back there. Last night it was down to 68 here. I had to put on a field jacket to sleep in.

Jerry went to school with a boy who was rescued on Luzon. Boy, was that a fast one we pulled on the Nips. So did (Admiral) Nimitz when he went to Tokyo. We are really going to town, Pappy. I mean to tell you, Pappy, it's rough, but we are getting them. In Europe, too, so all in all, things are O.K.

I just can't help but talk about Jerry. I meant to tell you, Pappy, she writes to me every day. I get more mail from her than any other guy in the outfit gets from their wife or sweetheart. Pappy, I think I am the luckiest guy in the world to have a swell wife like Jerry. Boy, what a baby we have! Gee, Pappy, when I think of what a swell Daddy and sisters and brothers I have, it makes me feel humble and thankful for all of you.

We are eating a lot of corn on the cob, about

twice a week. I hope we stay here for a while. Just what we need for about 8 weeks.

Things are really looking up now, Pappy. I have good news every day, and the Yanks are on the road to Tokyo and going full steam ahead.

Love, Your Son, Bill

Mindoro
Philippine Islands
APO 321
February 24, 1945

Hi, Pappy,

Jerry tells me you are giving me some competition with a Valentine. Seriously, Pappy, Jerry told me she thinks an awful lot of you. In fact, she likes everyone in our family and for that I am glad. I hope everyone likes her, too. You know, Pappy, someone told me that they think you have done a wonderful job of holding us together as a family. But then, you have always been a swell daddy to me.

Boy, Pappy, the month we have been here has done wonders for the outfit. The guys carry on like a bunch of kids. Up until we got the break of coming here where it's quiet we looked like we were about to crack.[12] I mean everyone was really worn out. But now since we got some good weeks of sleep and good chow and a chance to clean everything up we are ready to go for some more excitement.[13]

We have roasting ears about twice a week. Last week we had Jello—something I never thought we would have over here. But I guess wonders never cease. I never thought we would get a chance to rest up like this, either.

I got your Christmas package day before yesterday. The socks really came in handy and the soap was just in time. As for the eats, Pappy, I don't think you had better send any more eating stuff in a package—all the things were spoiled because it takes too long for it to get here.

I don't suppose I will ever get to see Manila. Something tells me we won't be one of the lucky outfits who will be there for the duration. I think we will wind up in the jungle someplace.

Thanks again for the package.

Your Son, Bill

At the Front 1942–1945

Battles had continued throughout Luzon in February, with more U.S. troops having landed on the island. Filipino and American resistance fighters also attacked Japanese positions and secured several locations. By early March the Allies had taken control of all strategically and economically important locations of Luzon. By March 1, the Manila Harbor, the finest in the East, was officially opened to Allied shipping.

Six days later, on March 7, General MacArthur returned to the island fortress he had been forced to leave three years before. "I see that the old flagpole still stands. Have your troops hoist the colors to its peak and let no enemy ever again haul it down," he proclaimed.

Corregidor was recaptured from the Japanese by March 1, 1945 followed by this flag-raising. (http://www.history.army.mil/brochures/luzon/pic3.jpg)

Okinawa

The last and largest of the Pacific Island battles of World War II, the Okinawa Campaign (March 1—June 22, 1945) involved the 287,000 troops of the U.S. Tenth Army against 130,000 soldiers of the Japanese Thirty-second Army. At stake were air bases vital to the projected invasion of Japan.

Iwo Jima, a barren volcanic island midway between Saipan and Japan and part of the Okinawa campaign, was considered desirable as an emergency base for United States B-29's flying to and from Japan. Cancellation of plans to take Taiwan provided an opportunity for the Central Pacific forces to undertake the previously unscheduled conquest of Iwo Jima. Two Marine divisions had made the assault on February 19, touching off a month of fighting. A third Marine division was then added, as 23,000 Japanese, firmly entrenched in terrain that gave them an advantage, resulted in the cost of some 20,000 American casualties for the tiny island. Then on March 16, 1945, the campaign came to an official end.

Mindoro
Philippine Islands
APO 321
March 23, 1945

Dear Pappy,

I am in the hospital recovering from an operation; they took out my appendix. I was only allowed to write once and that letter was to Jerry.

The surgeon who operated on me was tops. No kidding, Pappy, I really mean it. I have about a 2½ inch incision in my stomach where he cut to take my appendix out. They gave me a spinal and I was not even sick, not even a headache. The nurses here, too, are wonderful people. It's the first time since I left the States I have been around nurses. These nurses are better than the ones back there by far. Miss Bates is the nurse and Capt. Beck is the surgeon.

No kidding, Pappy, I really can't say enough about Capt. Beck and Miss Bates. I have had 3 or 4 nurses besides Miss Bates, but she was the best one. We have another young doctor and he, too, is tops. Capt. Beck had some years in civilian life. I wish I knew the young Captain's name but I do know about his work. He is the Ward Doctor of my Ward now. I am in 4F; that's the number of my Ward and so that makes me 4F.[14]

As to the orchard, Pappy, Jerry has some money in it and so she has the say. I will write and ask her. For my part if we can get a place next to the field where Skip[15] is, that's all right. I really wish I were home now, Pap. It's kind of hard to say. But I'll write and tell Jerry and see what she says. You see, Pappy, Jerry and I had really intended to build there someday when this war is over.

Tell Jerry to come over and talk about it. Show her and let her decide, because if she wants it, I want it, too. So you get together with her.

I did not want it for the orchard. I knew that was gone when I was in high school yet. One thing Pappy, make Slim [16] pay, no easy deal like before. Sis told me about you cashing war bonds to pay for it. I think I know Slim as well as you do. So, if Jerry says OK it is good enough for me.

Not much doing here in the hospital, just taking it easy. I sleep between sheets. I never saw them over here before I came in the hospital. I don't expect to see them after I get out [of the hospital], but I am enjoying it while it lasts.

When you get Eggy's new permanent address send it to me, please.

Good Luck, Bill

The Battle of Okinawa was one of the last major battles of WWII, and the Ryukyu Islands were the only inhabited part of Japan to experience a land battle during the War. The invasion of the Ryukyus by troops of the U.S. Tenth Army began on March 26, 1945 with the capture of small islands near Okinawa, where forward naval bases were then established. In preparation, the American troops had received a steady stream of reinforcements to construct elaborate fortifications, including countless concrete pillboxes and fortified positions, tank traps, and minefields.

The main landing on Okinawa had been set for April 1, 1945, Easter Sunday. (This date is sometimes used to mark the beginning of the Okinawa Campaign) and on the same date the 32nd Division of the Japanese Imperial Army was activated for duty on Okinawa. The day began and ended with the heaviest concentration of naval gunfire ever expended to support an amphibious landing.

The fighting lasted until June and here, for the first time, Americans were invading what the Japanese defenders considered their home soil, and the defense was fanatic in the extreme. After the Americans breached the Marianas' defense line in July, some 1,500 miles to the southeast, the defensive preparations accelerated, digging in at Shuri, Okinawa's second largest urban area. Shuri was also the cultural center and ancient royal capital of Okinawa. With civilians conscripted, the total defense force was approximately 100,000 Japanese souls.

Misled, the Americans had expected the Okinawan people to welcome them as liberators but instead the Okinawans were fearful of Americans. As a result of that fear, some Okinawans had joined militias and fought alongside the Japanese against the Americans. This was a major cause of the civilian casualties, as American military forces could not distinguish between combatants and civilians.

The American Tenth Army marshaled approximately 183,000 troops for the various assault phases. Almost 116,000 men in five divisions, all reinforced with tank and tractor battalions and attached service units, were assigned to make the initial landings.

However, American Army troops suffered heavy casualties, as did the Navy, when Japanese suicide flyers, the Kamikazes, sank some 25 American ships and damaged 165 others in a desperate attempt to save the Ryukyu Islands for Japan. In the end the Americans won the battle and the capture of the Ryukyus by the Americans erased any hope Japanese military leaders might have held that an invasion of the home islands could be averted.

By the end of the 82-day Okinawa campaign, which had begun, as noted, on Easter Sunday, April 1, 1945, Japan had lost more than 77,000 soldiers and the Allies had suffered more than 65,000 casualties—including 14,000 dead. The Japanese kamikaze attacks on the U.S. Navy were also successful; seven carriers were damaged and American casualties numbered between 12,000 and 14,000—the price America paid for winning this island, in addition to the nearly 7,000 Naval and Marine losses at Iwo Jima. However, this heartbreaking news was not released to the public.

Nearly ten inches of rain fell on Okinawa during the last ten days in May, slowing American progress and giving the remainder of the Japanese 32nd Army a chance to escape. Each retreating defender carried with him no more than a twenty-day ration and as much equipment and supplies as he could carry. In the southeast corner of the island, the Japanese defenders burrowed in for a final stand.

Because capture of the Ryukyus had given Allied naval and air forces excellent bases within 700 miles of Japan proper, Japan was subjected to increasingly intensive air attack and even to naval bombardment throughout June and July.

Allied forces were now in position for the final assault. In preparation for the invasion of mainland Japan itself, a reorganization of U.S. Pacific forces had been effected on April 3, 1945 when General MacArthur was given command of all Army forces and Admiral Nimitz of all Naval forces. MacArthur's new command was designated U.S. Army Forces, Pacific (AFPAC). However, the war ended before the reorganization could have any effect on operations.

The capture of the Ryukyu Islands by the Allies had already erased any hope Japanese military leaders might have held that an invasion of the home islands could be averted.

Another indication was that long before the firing stopped on Okinawa, engineers and construction battalions, following close on the heels of the combat forces, had transformed the island into a major base for the projected invasion of the Japanese home islands. A soldier walking back over the terrain for which he had fought so hard just weeks before might not have recognized the landscape, as hills were leveled, ravines filled, and water courses altered to make way for airstrips, highways, and ammunition dumps. (This would have been the assignment of which Bill Calhoon was a part.)

Mindoro
Philippine Islands
APO 321
April 1, 1945

Dear Pappy,

Jerry told me Leroy Shultz has been killed in action. She said his mother is really taking it hard. Wish I could write and explain how sorry I am to hear it, but every time I start to write I start out all wrong.

I don't know how Jerry decided about the orchard field, but whichever way she said, it's ok by me.

I am going back to baking next week. Up till now I have been pulling area guard. It's the easiest duty, so guys that are just getting over sickness pull that duty.

No kidding, Pappy, the operation was perfect and, as for the treatment, I can only say it was tops. If I would have paid the bill I could not have asked to be treated any better, so for that you can be thankful because I know you must have wondered how I was making out.

It's quiet around here, even worse than Guinea. Boy, it's as dead here as Middletown used to be at 3:00 in the morning.

I am going to Easter Sunrise Service in the morning. Since this place has become a back area,[7] we have time to have some beautiful church services.

Looks like Hitler will soon have to quit. Boy, I hope they send all the planes that are used over there, over here on the double. We have done pretty good, but, damn, I hope it's soon over. Boy, how I would like to see Jerry and Butch and all of you again.

No ham and eggs tomorrow, but I guess we can't have everything. We do have tomatoes fairly often. Watch the St. Louis Cards go, Pappy!

Bill

The Death of President Roosevelt

Even as German resistance crumbled and victory appeared certain, President Roosevelt, returning in February 1945 a sick man from the Yalta conference of the Combined Chiefs of Staff, went to his winter home in Warm Springs, Georgia, to prepare for the inauguration of the United Nations at San Francisco. On April 12, as the President was drafting a Jefferson Day address, he suffered a cerebral hemorrhage which brought instant death. The nation mourned.

That evening (April 12) the presidential train, bearing the President's body, began its journey home to Washington where it arrived the following morning. With little delay the funeral procession, with the casket on a black-draped caisson drawn by six white horses, proceeded to the White House. Just before four o'clock, a thunderstorm moved into the city, the streets fell dark, and hard rain pelted down; then, as suddenly as it had come, the black cloud moved away.

Promptly at 4:00 p.m. every public activity ceased and nearly every person in the country stood in silence for the funeral. Radios fell silent; all telephone service halted, and the teletypes clicked out the word "SILENCE" over and over.

Subway trains came to a standstill, and the passengers bowed their heads. On a trolley in Times Square the passengers stood in tribute, while nearby pedestrians knelt in honor where they were in front of the out-of-town newspaper stand. The following day the body of the President was borne to Hyde Park for burial in his mother's rose garden.

Chief Justice Harlan F. Stone administering the oath of office to Harry S. Truman in the Cabinet Room of the White House, April 12, 1945 Repository, Library of Congress Prints and Photographs Division, Washington, DC, 20540.

Within the next three weeks of the death of President Roosevelt, Italian partisans killed Mussolini (April 28), Hitler committed suicide (April 30), Berlin surrendered to Russia (May 2), and Germany signed an unconditional surrender (May 7). Thus, the war came to an end in the West.

Mindoro
Philippine Islands
APO 321
April 13, 1945

(Because of the time zones, this would be USA April 12, and obviously Bill Calhoon had not yet heard of the death of President Roosevelt or the fall of Berlin prior to sending this letter.)

Hi, Pappy,

At last we have found a good swimming hole. First fresh water swimming we have had in about a year. In all the other places it has been salt water. We have a diving board and you don't have to worry about touching bottom if you dive a little deep.

We won a ball game today. First one I played since I came out of the hospital. Felt good to play ball again.

We are allowed to wear shorts around camp and, as a result, I am getting back my suntan I lost while I was in the hospital.

To show how we do things over here, I'll tell you the story of how I got my shorts. Down in Guinea an Australian wanted some kind of souvenir from the States. I knew some guys who had just come across [the Pacific Ocean]. They wanted a knife, so from one of them I bought a watch for £1½ Australian money. Then I went to the Aussie and traded him the watch for a knife and the pair of shorts. I sold the knife to the guy fresh from the States for £3 Aussie money. So, on the deal I received £1½ and the shorts.

According to the news, the Yanks are once more on the move for Berlin. Hope they make it this try.

If you find out what is the matter with Eggy, let me know please!

Pappy, I can't get you any souvenirs here. I'll have to wait until we hit one of the large cities so please be patient and I will try my darnedest to get something for you.

Mail is kind of poor right now; should have a lot one of these days.

A furlough to the States has been increased from 30 to 45 days. Boy, if they only step up our quota, I may make it before the war is over.

I sent Jerry some pictures. I only wish I could get some more made. But it's impossible, so I guess I'll have to wait until things get better over here.

Tell Helen I got her letter yesterday but I can't answer it right now.

Love, Bill

Mindoro
Philippine Islands
APO 321
April 24, 1945

Hi, Pappy,

Jerry has told me about the orchard. She said to get rid of it, so I know you have proceeded to do so. She said it's all right, so it's all right. By my own confession, Pappy, it looks like I let Jerry do my talking but I know she's OK, so she's OK.

I'm catching on to baking a little now, and so I guess if the war lasts about ten years yet, I'll be a baker maybe. I hope it's over and long gone by that time.

Things are popping these days for the Navy, so I guess there's not much time for Clam to look around to find me; the same goes for Glen.

I got a letter from Pud yesterday, but it must have been delayed somewhere because the date on it was November 14 which has been here and gone quite a while.

This place here is deader than Guinea ever was. All you do in this place is work and hit the sack. I mean my sack really gets used a lot here at this place.

Yesterday I got a letter from Jerry dated April 12. I think that's pretty quick service, don't you?

There's a guy on this island who says he knows me, but I can't find any trace of him. Maybe his outfit has pulled out.

Here's hoping that Pud and Eggie, with a little help from the rest of the Army, soon make the Nazis throw in the towel.

I think I'm doing fine with a little help from Glen, Cal, and a few more, as we got the Nips a little scared.

God Bless you Pappy. Your Son, Bill

Meritorious Unit Commendation

Clark Field, Luzon
APO 74
May 7, 1945

Hi, Pappy,

I have started to cook now. It's not a bad job. The only thing is that every other morning I have to get up at 3:30 and that is rough.

The day before yesterday we (those who are in my company) were awarded the Meritorious Unit Plaque. We are the first company in the Pacific to be awarded the plaque.

We went to the 5th Air Force Headquarters. The place was (and is) a permanent base to have a commanding general and a band over here, so it must be important as we had both. To beat even this, I was amazed because when we marched to the general's headquarters we went in military order and in step. Each and every man in the company—and it was the first time in two years we had marched with a band. We kept in step. I would not have believed it if I had not seen it—and been a part of it.

The place we went was a beautiful place and

one you have often heard of. Even now after the two battles you can see how beautiful it must have been. (Note: This likely would have been Clark Air Field on Luzon as it was the 5th Air Force Headquarters with a commanding general and its own band.)

Honest, Pappy, I'm proud of this award. I could get only one copy of the order so if you want to see it, ask Jerry for it. It's the highest award a service unit can get. I don't ever remember of a service unit getting a presidential citation, so we had reached the heights with this award.

I'm very tired and I have to work tomorrow morning so I had better quit.

Your Son, Bill

Editor's Note: This verifies the recollection by the Calhoon family that their father had been part of the unit that helped build airfields and provide other tactical support. It also explains why their father (as well as all others in the service) could NOT reveal in letters what their military duties entailed. It would be easy to read through these letters, and those of other military men, and mistakenly think that "they didn't have it so bad." It is in the research on the stories behind the letters that unveils the extraordinary efforts all gave, both on and off the battle field.

This information further places William Calhoon's unit as a subsidiary—or support unit—of the 5th Air Force.

5th Air Force
APO 710 [18]
May 17, 1945

Hi, Pappy,

The company has been cut in half. Ever since we hit here last month we have been moving and splitting up. Instead of one two-hundred man outfit we are now two 121-man outfits. Bill Wallace, the guy who came in with me, is in the new outfit. It's the 1400th MP Company. Most of the guys I worked with are in the new company.

After two years over here they broke us up. But that's the way it is, so that is the way it will be.

It's civilization, concrete roads, parade ground, ball fields. Two swimming pools and even in some places running cold water. The only trouble is we are going to be GI [19] in a little while and, believe me, Pappy, that's going to be hard. [To the enlisted men themselves "G.I." did not have the connotation of enlisted military G.I.; Rather, Pfc. Calhoon is using this term satirically. See endnote.]

With all of the comforts and beautiful places we have, I guess I'm what they call a bush man; that is, I don't want to be a garrison [20] soldier as long as we are over here. I would much rather climb on a L.S.T.[21] and go on another invasion. I know I've told you I was tired of front line duty, but I think it's lots better than to be dressed up all the time and pretty soon you will have to salute every second lieutenant you see.

From what I know I believe everyone in the company feels the same. It's a lot nicer to run around in any kind of clothes you feel like. No wonder people connected with headquarters look so white.[22] There, they have to wear a shirt all the time. Boy, Pappy, it's going to be rough wearing a shirt all the time. I don't like it, but I know I'm doing it.

I am a cook now. Seems like they want a cook worse than a baker, so now I am cooking. Like it pretty good. Get enough to eat, anyhow.

Love, Your Son, Bill

5th Air Force
APO 710
May 24, 1945

Hi, Pappy,

I'm quite ashamed for not writing to tell you I am still O.K. I am a cook now. They broke up my old outfit and made two M.P. companies out of it. Bill Wallace, the guy from Hershey who came in with me, is in the new outfit.

We are going to be garrison soldiers for a while. I doubt if I see any real combat for quite a while.

Boy, how we have worked since we hit this place. We had just started on a camp area when orders came through to break up the outfit. We were the ones to move, the new company was the one to stay. Now we are building a new camp area. We are at a peacetime post. Nothing much is left, but just enough to realize how beautiful a place it was at one time.

Already we have formal retreat twice a week. If they want us to be garrison soldiers they should send us back to the States. But I guess it won't kill me. It's kind of nice to sit away from air raids.

This place sure beats Guinea. At least the people here speak English. There are some nice towns, too, but not much is left.

We do have plenty of ball diamonds around here so when camp is set up we should be able to get some ball playing in. Baseball games, not softball. Boy, does it sound good to hear the bat crack out a double.

I think I'll get back to the States in about a year or 14 months. I believe we will start on the Nips right soon; at least I hope so.

I guess Cal is in the thick of it about this time. Boy, they are really giving Tojo hell and they are going to catch more as time goes by.

I lost Eggy's address; please send it to me again.[23]

On the bulletin board today was a Letter of Commendation from General Arnold. Commanding General of the U.S.A.A.F. to the 5th Air Force, so again the 5th A.F. is on the ball.

Chow is pretty good now. But every now and then we hit it rough for a day or two.

The Nazis have quit so maybe Pud will get back to the States. He's been over a long time and he sure deserves a break.

I have to get up at 3:30 a.m. to go on duty. So, as soon as the breaks come my way, I'll tell you about how long I'll have to stay over on this side of the ocean. I hope it looks like I'm good for a while yet.

Your Son, Bill

Somewhere on Luzon
APO 710

June 7, 1945

Dear Pappy,

Sorry I can't get a couple of weeks off right now. Sort of busy[24], but maybe Pud can get home to help you.

Kind of tough for Eggy, but, believe me, Pap, I know they will give him the best of care.

The ball fever has hit the company again, so yesterday we went out and had a workout for about 3½ hours. Not a bit sore today, so I guess I'm still in fair shape.

I really believe President Truman will try to keep his promise. I don't say he can fill Roosevelt's shoes, but I believe he will try his damnedest and that's all any of us can do.

Had a letter from Pud today, but it was dated in March so he did not say if he was coming home or not.

Jerry told me about the candlelight service and it must have been very beautiful.[25]

Chow is pretty good right now. Tomorrow we have fresh butter and fresh hamburger.

Pappy, I know you want souvenirs, but the prices are terrific beyond words. For a handkerchief they want 12 pesos which is six bucks. If I can, I promise you something. I am sending a coin along, I hope it will do until I get something better.[26]

I realize as never before, Daddy, just how much I have to come home to. Makes a person a little more careful when he is in a nice warm spot. I know I have the sweetest wife and baby in the world. Believe me, Pappy, it helps when you realize you have someone like that back there.[27]

Afraid there's not much chance of getting home in '45 anymore, but I should make it in '46 for sure.[28]

I see where the Cards are in third place. Put your money on them Pap. They will take the pennant again.

Bill

Somewhere on Luzon
APO 710
June 13, 1945

Hi, Pappy,

Jerry told me that Pud is on his way home. I sure hope so. He's been over there long enough.

Things are looking better over here. The last two days chow has been kind of rough, but we were getting fresh meat every day. Hamburger steak and once or twice fresh eggs.

Boy, Pappy, talk about high prices; never have I seen anything to equal prices over here. I'd like very much to send something home but prices are too high.

I have 85 points, enough to get out. But the Air Forces will be the last ones out, so I figure in about another year I should hit the trail to the States.[29] Hope it's sooner, but right now I don't believe it will be sooner.

The place is OK now. Not too G.I.[30] yet. Good shows and plenty of ball games. Our guys pull duty 24 hours a day, so we can't get enough at one time to form a team.

I'm working nights now. Not much to do, because right now we don't get any flour; when we get flour I have to bake. Right now all I have to do is make coffee for the guys who go on at midnight, about a half hour's work. Sometimes I have to mix flap jack batter or to par boil bacon. It's really the best job I've had in a long time. I guess it won't last long, but who cares?

Tell Pud to write if he hits the States pretty soon.

The rainy season is here again. But it's a part of my life now and I really don't mind it. Getting wet over here is as common as being dry, that is, during the rainy season. Our tent leaks even if it is new. But I can still sleep.

I was downtown today and had my picture taken. I'm going to send the picture and negative. When I send them I'll tell Jerry to have some copies made.

I'll have to get the stove going, so that will be all for this time.

Your Son, Bill

Somewhere on Luzon
APO 710
June 16, 1945

Hi, Pappy,

We have a sweet set up at this place, Daddy. Showers, swimming pool, stage, and we have some really fine stage productions. A lot of Filipino stage shows. It's by far the best place we hit since we left the States. Sometimes it gets rough, but not half as rough as when Tojo comes calling. It's been a long time since the Nips have come over. There are still stray Nips around and often you can hear small arms fire. Every now and then they bring some here to the stockade. It's really getting garrison[31] around here. There's a base order out effective yesterday: We will salute. There will be no close order drills.

Henry Aldrich is on the radio.

Glad to hear Eggie is O.K. Kind of bad about him going over when he was unfit for service. We all make mistakes, Pappy. I know he was in no shape to come in, but there was nothing we could do or say except to be proud of him. Let's hope he gets out now.

Yah, Pappy, I'm proud of my outfit and of the unit decoration. I know damn well we earned it. I might be an Air Corps Commando, but it was no picnic. We have it nice now, but I'm sure it won't last for the duration.

The first guy is leaving on points tomorrow for the good old States. He has 107 points so he's on his way.

Jerry told me all about the candlelight service. It must have been very beautiful indeed.

As for the cooking, Pappy, most of the stuff over here is dehydrated. I doubt very much if I shall cook when I come home; in fact, I know I won't.

Pap, I hope you are right about the Nips folding up. For my personal opinion, which is not worth much, I say 18 months yet. We still have to invade Japan and that is not going to be a pushover, believe me.

I hope I get back sooner, but I believe I'll have about 26 months in before I get back.[32]

I guess Cal is up where it's plenty rough and, boy, what a job the boys in the Navy are doing.

I have to go to work now, Pappy. Please inform your daughter-in-law that your son Bill *has no intention of cooking his own meals when he is once again a John Q Civilian.*

The first American-built airfield on Okinawa, a 7,000-foot airstrip at Yontan, just east of the invasion beaches, was operational by June 17, 1945. By the end of the month a total of five air bases were ready for the heavy bombers that could soften up the islands of Kyushu and Honshu for the invasion that everyone believed inevitable. Operationally, the campaign for the Ryukyus had succeeded in its mission.

Among the nearly 35,000 American casualties were General Buckner, who was killed on June 18. He was succeeded by Maj. Gen. Roy S. Geiger, who was in turn succeeded by General Joseph W. Stilwell, who arrived to assume command of the Tenth Army on June 22.

Finally, on July 2 America's bloodiest campaign against Imperial Japan formally ended.

In July, after meeting at Potsdam, President Truman and Prime Minister Winston Churchill presented Japan with an ultimatum to surrender. The alternative, Japan was told, would be "prompt and utter destruction."[33] Japan refused to acknowledge this Potsdam Declaration, and on July 25, 1945 the United States gave the order for the dropping of atomic bombs. However, information about this order was not generally known and certainly not announced to anyone. Only those involved in the mission had any idea of its importance and risk, and even they knew little.

Letters written home continued as normal.

Western Pacific
APO 710
July 24, 1945

Hi, Pappy,

How's Bud these days? I guess he's one happy boy from what Jerry tells me.

This place I hate worse than Guinea. Talk about dead! This beats Middletown or even Bainbridge or Falmouth.

Today we were supposed to have a ball game, but something got all snafu.[34] When we got to the diamond two teams were playing so we had to come back.

Two guys left for the States today on points. [See below] Both of them were in the outfit since '43 down in Mobile. They were really happy. They left here by plane to a back area to where they got a ship for home. Home. Boy, how I miss that place. With a lot of luck perhaps I'll get back in 10 or 12 months.[35]

Chow is kind of rough, but perhaps it will get better. Mail is pretty good. Every time we have mail call there's sure to be a letter from Jerry, and that is good for my morale. I hear from everyone in the family regularly.

I saw some combat film [produced by the military] tonight and somehow I like them pretty much. They show how the rest of the Army is doing. Every now and then I see pictures of places I've been.

Cal must be seeing plenty of action these days. The Navy is really doing a super swell job.

Jerry says Edgar has it made now and that Europe is good.

I have 85 points—number 15 to leave for the States. So far as I can see I have a long wait yet before I leave.

Tell Pud to write and tell me what it's like to be an ex-soldier.

Love, Your Son, Bill

The End of the War

On August 6 the first atomic bomb was dropped on Hiroshima, wiping out the Second Japanese Army, razing four square miles of the city, and killing 60,175 persons. Three days later, a few hours after Russia had declared war on Japan, the second bomb exploded over Nagasaki, killing 36,000 persons, most of them civilians. Emperor Hirohito surrendered on August 14 ending the war in the Pacific.

A little after noon Japan Standard Time on August 15, 1945, Emperor Hirohito's announcement of Japan's acceptance of the terms of the Potsdam Declaration was broadcast to the Japanese people over the radio. Earlier the same day, the Japanese government had broadcast an announcement over Radio Tokyo that "acceptance of the Potsdam Proclamation [would be] coming soon," and had advised the Allies of the surrender by sending a cable to U.S. President Harry S. Truman via the Swiss diplomatic mission in Washington, DC.

A broadcast by Truman was aired at seven p.m. (daylight time in Washington, DC) on August 14 announcing the communication and that the formal signing event was scheduled for September 2. In his announcement of Japan's surrender on August 14, Truman said that "the proclamation of V-J Day must wait upon the formal signing of the surrender terms by Japan."

There is no way to know when the soldiers themselves were informed about the surrender. It is likely that they would have heard about the major event of the first atomic bombs on August 6 and August 9, and were told not to include this in their letters home. Even though the event of a surrender would have been huge, Bill, following orders, in several letters says only "if the war is over."

The nuclear bombing of Hiroshima and Nagasaki provided an unexpected quickening in the pace of demobilization. Nonetheless, the best plans were still complicated by the need for the U.S. military to remain in place for peace-keeping duty. Regardless of the delays, everyone focused on coming home—whatever that might mean for each individual—to a steady routine of life where even the mail was delivered on schedule, twice a day.

Thus, a little more than a month after the campaign ended, it was with intense joy that the weary soldiers and marines who carried the fight through the mud and over the rough terrain of Okinawa learned that they would <u>not</u> have to face a final climactic battle. The Japanese formally surrendered on September 2, 1945, and the campaign of the Ryukyus was remembered as the last major battle of World War II for the American soldier.

Still pockets of Japanese soldiers held out in the mountains with most of them ceasing resistance because of the unconditional surrender of Japan. However, a scattered few of them held out for many years afterwards.

Casualties were stunningly high for the Japanese. Japanese losses were 205,535 dead, with 9,050 taken prisoners. Allied losses were far lower, with 8,310 dead and 29,560 wounded.

The surrender did not, however, mean that all the troops would come home immediately nor that others would not be sent overseas as part of their tour of duty.

As just one example of thousands of young men, early that spring Eugene Bloom, much to his mother's dismay, had enlisted in the Navy, having idolized his cousin Johnny Wayne who had been part of the Leyte battle. At the time of Eugene's enlistment the war was by no means over and even should it soon end there was no guarantee that harm would not come to him.

Eugene, however, had two purposes in choosing to enlist: one, the draft was still in effect and by enlisting he had a choice in the branch of service he selected, and, two, the GI Bill (Servicemen's Readjustment Act), which had been enacted in 1944, would pay for his college education following his military service. He knew that his parents would find it a financial hardship to send him to college and it made sense to him to enlist, get his service time over with, get a college education, marry his sweetheart, and get on with his life.

Eugene's mother was heartbroken when her second son, a year younger, said he also planned to follow the same pathway as his brother had taken as soon as he was graduated. There was little their mother could say, knowing this scene had been played in thousands of homes since 1941. This is only one example of the sacrifice of many families and the young men who interrupted their lives to serve their country.

POINT SYSTEM USED FOR THE EUROPEAN THEATRE

On May 10, 1945, two days after the unconditional surrender of Germany to the allies on VE Day, the War Department announced a point system for the demobilization and discharge of Army and Army Air Force enlisted personnel. The point system, called the Advanced Service Rating Score, had the objective of achieving equity in the demobilization. Soldiers were given one point for each month of military service and one additional point was given for each month of overseas service. Each battle star or decoration earned a soldier five points. Soldiers were awarded 12 points per dependent child up to a maximum of three children. A total of 85 points was needed for eligibility. Soldiers who had earned that number of points were to be demobilized as soon as transport back to the United States was available.

POINT SYSTEM USED FOR THE PACIFIC THEATRE

On VJ Day slightly more than 12 millionAmerican men and women were serving in the military with approximately 7 million of them in foreign countries or at sea. Deciding the best and fairest way to discharge individuals was debated among the military leadership until it was suggested to ask the men themselves. The results led to the order of discharge based first on overseas service, followed by number of dependents and then time in the military and age of the individual. This plan offered the servicemen the first faint promise of "coming home." A Gallup poll in June 1945 reported that 73 percent of the public felt the established point system to be fair.

Somewhere in the Ryukyu Islands
APO 710
August 8, 1945

Dear Daddy,

I received a letter from you today and in it was a question I find hard to answer. You asked me if I wanted to come home. I want to get out as soon as I can. I'll try to explain why I won't be home for perhaps another year.

I am number 15 on the list to come home, at one or two at month, being discharged from our unit, so you can see it's a long time yet. Air Force men in the Pacific will be among the last to leave and we are part of their support services. Like everything else in the service you must wait until your turn comes.

Even if I get back to the States it does not mean I will be discharged. Some of the boys who went home on forward deployment are not coming back but they are staying in the service. MPs, I believe, are essential because of all the boys coming back at the same time the MPs are needed over here.

So, Pap, I want you to know I won't be home for quite some time and even if I get back to the states it does not mean I will get discharged. Don't get it into your head I should get home because I have 85 points. There are lots of guys with 100 points who are not started back yet. I guess, Pappy, you don't know much about the point system. It's not your fault because, after all, you are not in the service.

It doesn't mean everyone with 85 points or better will soon be home. It takes a long time to do these things. Sure, I want to get out, but I still have a lot of time to spend over here. I hate it, but I know it must be done. So, Pappy, I must tell you this. I don't think there's much chance of spending Christmas at home. I may make it for Easter but I won't bet on it. I'll bet Jerry never told you that I'll be home soon, did she?

Who did Abe Derr get married to? In one of Jerry's letters today she said he had got married, but she did not know who he married.

I lost some hair, Pap, but I'm far from catching up with you. Remember, Pappy, when I get back I think I'll buy a wig for you so you look like your son when you go to see Rosey.

I am going to hit the sack now. That's bed to you, so I'll say good-bye for now.

Love, Bill

APO 710
August 14, 1945

Dear Pappy,

I think our job is about over out here in the Pacific. At least I hope so.

There are some bad points to being in the MPs and I think perhaps I'll know for sure. So even if the war is over, I know I'll never get home as quick as Sud did, so don't look for me until I tell you I'm on my way back. One thing you can be sure of, Pap, I'm not going to stay over here any longer than I have to, so if I stay a while it's because I have to, not because I want to.

Tonight the quartermaster called up so we went down and got fresh eggs, fresh apples, fresh spinach and fresh fish. Boy, tomorrow we will put on a real feast.

Gee, Pap, if the war is over, and I don't know if it is or not,[36] that means no more air raids. That's really something, no more air raids. Hurrah! Better yet, it means I will soon be home with Jerry and our son. By soon I mean five or six months. That's not long compared to the three years I've been away. I'm not even sure if I shall be able to get my old job back, but who cares. Just as long as I can see everyone, I guess I'll have time to worry when I get back. Just now, I'm hoping the war is really over.

I had a letter from Edgar today; he seems to like his job pretty well.

I guess I can't write anymore right now, Pappy. I'm so darn happy I can't even think straight. If the war is over, I'm happy, and, if it's not, I guess I just sweat it out for a while longer.

Love, Your Son, Bill

We can almost feel Bill's excitement, yet hesitancy to say he heard—or knew—that the war was over. On this day, August 14, 1945, the day Bill wrote his letter, the Japanese government cabled to the United States their surrender. The following day, August 15, 1945, news of the surrender was announced to the world, but no doubt the military personnel in the Philippines knew.

Okinawa
APO 710
August 18, 1945

Dear Pappy,

Well, the war is over[37] so in three or four months I should be heading for the good United States of America. I'm almost sure it will be a good three months. It won't be long until I know just about when I'll be heading there.

Meanwhile I think our chow will get better now. Tomorrow we have ham. I guess it will stay good now, at least I hope so.

Best of all, we shall have no more air raids, and believe me, I'm really glad for that. Unless you've been through a lot of real ones, you can never know what it's like. I'm thankful you never had to go through it.

I really don't know what I am going to do, and even now that I know I'll be getting home, I still can't find myself worrying about it.

Believe me, Dad, the only thing I'm worried about is seeing Jerry again and Butch, our son. Guess this army taught me that the only important thing in this life is to be happy. I don't think it will take much to make me happy.

I don't think it's much use to send me any Christmas packages. I believe I'll be on the way by then.

Your Son, Bill

Somewhere on Okinawa
APO 710
August 28, 1945

Dear Daddy,

I wish I could say I'll be headed for the States, but it will be awhile yet. We still go by points and I'm No. 14 on the list. At one or two or even three a month, figure it out for yourself.

I guess we are going to garrison life. We need to sew on our 5th Air Force patches and start to shave every day, as well as wear proper uniforms and that sort of stuff.

We have been seeing some swell shows here of late. "The Southerner," "Eagle Squadron," "Cover Girl," and a lot of combat shorts[38] by the army combat camera crews. The G. I. Combos[39] beat the Hollywood stuff to hell and back, believe me.

Chow is sometimes good, sometimes bad, mostly kind of bad.

Our radio is working all the time and, boy, that is really swell!

We've come a long way, Pap, and still have a way to go. But it's a lot easier now. Just a matter of months—not years—anymore.

Love, Your Son, Bill

Five days after Bill had written this letter, on September 2, 1945, a formal surrender ceremony was held in Tokyo Bay aboard the USS Missouri. It was this date that President Truman declared to be VJ Day.

Homeward Bound

As early as mid-1943, the United States Army had recognized that, once victory was won, bringing the troops home would be a priority. Twelve million Americans were in uniform; and more than eight million of them were scattered across 55 theaters of war worldwide. Army Chief of Staff General George Marshall established committees to address the logistical problem. Eventually organization of the operation was given to the War Shipping Administration (WSA). It established and coordinated what was termed Operation Magic Carpet.

As the war came to a conclusion a major factor in arranging for the troops to "go home" was the problem of transportation. There simply were not enough ships to speedily accommodate the millions of military personnel who were to be discharged. Further it would not have been a wise military decision to not leave military in the areas now conquered. Therefore, a workable plan had to be devised quickly. While the troops had "come over" from the states in large numbers, they were not all deployed at the same time. They also could not all return at the same time.

Ships had been assigned and reassigned constantly during WWII, and at its peak, there were 65 large troopships in operation. These troop ships came from various sources; some were Navy owned, others Army-owned, and at least one Air Force-owned ship; others were bareboat charter, sub-bareboat charter, or on loan. Many were manned by civilian crews, employed under Civil Service regulations and carried on the rolls at the home ports of vessels. Some military members of ships' crews were in an administrative capacity—and in other cases the crews were furnished by the US Coast Guard, while others were contractor employed personnel.

However, the ships most available to transport troops home turned out to be those awkward workhorses—the Liberty ships—that seemed to have risen to meet almost every need of the entire war. Even though it had been recommended for years that the Liberty ships be withdrawn from service, the military needs required their continued use—and that intense need for troopship transport continued into the immediate postwar period in order to return troops from overseas to the United States as quickly as possible.

As noted in the first section of this book, the Department of the Army in 1951 destroyed all passenger lists, manifests, logs of vessels, and troop movement files of United States Army Transports for World War II. Thus, there is no longer an official record of who sailed on what ship. However, as near as can be determined, William H. Calhoon was aboard a troopship, heading home by the middle or third week of September.

The best guess is that if Bill had been aboard one of the larger ships—which is highly likely for such a distance, he would have left the Marshall Islands on **September 9, 1945** on the *George M. Randall*, carrying approximately 6,000 returnees, and landing on **September 22, 1945** at San Francisco, where he had started this long journey.[40]

While on his way home to a formal and honorable discharge—and proud of his service, Bill Calhoon's heart no doubt was pounding during the two weeks it took for the troop ship, with possibly thousands of other men, to cross the Pacific Ocean.

The end of the war in 1945 brought many soldiers home, but they did not return to the prosperous America that had been in existence during the war time. The economy had profited greatly from the war, but now that it was over, the thousands of jobs—that had been created for the war effort—disappeared and America's economy suffered (albeit short term) because of it. A major factor is that because of the sudden dropping of the bombs on Hiroshima and Nagasaki, the war ended more quickly than expected and the economy had not yet caught up with that major change. America wasn't quite ready for reconversion.

This situation thus forced the Truman administration to return America's economy to normal, turning thoughts from defense to a plan to rebuild. America needed to welcome its boys home with a promise of a bright future, rather than one of facing economic troubles.

Hummelstown was a microcosm of what was happening throughout the entire country where thousands upon thousands of men and women began to return home—some to resume their lives and some to discover that home as they remembered it no longer existed, because they had changed, people they knew had changed, or the town had changed. Most veterans headed home with the goal to create a better life, assisted in some part by a grateful nation. Jobs soon were waiting for the majority of the veterans and life in the many small towns offered some normalcy.

Those who wished to return to their families and jobs for the most part could do that and those who wanted to continue their education could do that—both because of the GI bill. The Servicemen's Readjustment Act of 1944 was created to provide opportunities to veterans. Those who wanted could attend college and those with families could find financial aid in purchasing a house or starting a business. This is what made it possible for Bill and Jerry to purchase their own home shortly after he had returned.

In a few areas there were problems finding jobs, even though many employers sincerely wanted to "hire a veteran" as the patriotic position. Truman's Fair Deal successfully raised the minimum wage from 40 cents to 75 cents an hour and also led to an expansion in Social Security benefits, both actions favorable to the economy. The country was, for the most part, united in these new plans.

Overall there was a feeling of great optimism. Most people were simply minding their own business, glad to welcome America's sons home, and helping each other—feeling normal. Most citizens said they felt that Americans were all united.

Surprisingly to many, however, was that most of the returning men said that despite the welcome home they did not think they had been heroic. Most said they believed they were just doing their job, expressing that the ones who were heroes were the ones who had made the ultimate sacrifice and could not come home.

Home

In late September after landing in San Francisco, from which he had been deployed May 30, 1943, Bill likely crossed the United States by train. He arrived at Fort Dix, New Jersey at the beginning of October.

On October 6, 1945 William H. Calhoon was honorably discharged from the military service of the United States of America at Fort Dix, New Jersey, three years after his Date of Entry into Active Service on November 19, 1942.

Hopping a bus to Pennsylvania, Bill arrived at the bus terminal in Harrisburg where a friend of the family picked him up and took him home where Jerry and his son Billy were waiting.

For a short time Bill and Jerry Calhoon lived with Jerry's parents while they made more specific future plans. Bill returned to work at the Hershey Company and began a spontaneous—

almost instinctive—practice to get to know his son. Almost every evening Bill could be seen wheeling his two-and-a-half-year-old son in a stroller, walking through the neighborhood streets of Hummelstown, greeting neighbors and quietly conversing with Billy, calling the little boy's attention to whatever they passed. This was paternal bonding before anyone had a name for it.

Within a year Bill and Jerry began to initiate the plans they had been talking about for three years through letters and soon purchased a house on North Lingle Avenue at the west end of Hershey. There they began life together as their own family unit—everything that Bill had dreamed of in the Philippines.

Postscript

In mid-November, about six weeks after Bill had come home, Pap received a letter from his son Clarence (Clem), the only letter from Clarence still in possession of the family. Clem had enlisted in the service (the only son to serve in the Navy) in the early summer of 1943, at age 32—ten years older than his brother Bill. The two brothers kept missing each other at various outposts even though both were serving in the Philippines Campaign. They did, however, correspond, as Bill had noted in his letters he had written home while in the service.

From Clarence:

October 17, 1945

Dear Dad and Family,

Here are a few lines to let you know that I am still O.K. I hope you are all well and getting along fine back home there. Well, it looks like I may be on my way back soon. I got examined and signed a couple of papers. I sure hope it is before we pull out of Okinawa this time.

We changed captains again yesterday and had inspection. If they were all like the other old man[41] this wouldn't be so bad, but I don't know what this fellow is like. I sure hope I am not on long enough to find out. You may as well not write anymore until you hear from me again. Well, that is about all for now. I hope to see you very soon.

May God Bless You All, Clarence

And presumably the family did see Clarence soon. He came home before the end of the year but did not tell anyone the date of his expected homecoming. He just walked in the door, saying, "Pap, I'm home."

Pap offered a prayer as each of his sons came home. He had never considered himself special, just a God-loving man who had done his own tour of duty by holding together his family of eight children, sending four sons to war, praying for them, writing faithfully to them, and welcoming each one home again.

Appendices

Military Campaigns and Awards

1127ᵗʰ Military Police Company, Aviation

Participated in the following Campaigns of World War II as part of the USAAF Fifth Air Force:

New Guinea	January 24, 1943 — December 31, 1944
Leyte	October 17, 1944 — July 1, 1945
Luzon	December 15, 1944 — July 4, 1945

The 1127th Military Police Company, Fifth Air Force had combat zone responsibilities strikingly different from the law enforcement duties conventionally associated with the Military Police Corps. Their responsibilities more closely resembled mission loads traditionally assigned to infantry units. These responsibilities consisted of, but were not limited to, patrols including mounted and dismounted patrols as well as LP/OP (Listening Post/Observation Post) "static patrols," movement to contact, route reconnaissance, raids, cordon and search operations, and convoy and personnel escorts.

Operationally, these duties fell under the "area security" and "maneuver and mobility support" operational categories of the main functions of the Military Police Corps.[1]

https://www.usamilitarymedals.com/products/military-police-regimental-corps-crest

http://search.aol.com/aol/image?q=military-police-regimental-corps-crest&v_t=client97_inbox

---

[1] http://www.allexperts.com/ep/669-116358/Military-History/Richard-V-Horrell.htm

Meritorious Unit Commendation

The Meritorious Unit Commendation was awarded to units for exceptionally meritorious conduct in performance of outstanding services for at least six continuous months during the period of military operations against an armed enemy occurring on or after January 1, 1944. Service in a combat zone was not required, but it had to be directly related to the combat effort. The unit must have displayed such outstanding devotion and superior performance of exceptionally difficult tasks as to set it apart and above other units with similar missions.

The degree of achievement required was the same as that which would warrant award of the Legion of Merit to an individual. For services performed during World War II, awards were made only to service units and only for services performed between January 1, 1944 and September 15, 1946.

The Meritorious Service Unit Plaque was established by War Department Circular No. 345, dated August 23, 1944. The circular provided that military personnel assigned or attached to an organization were entitled to wear the Meritorious Service Unit Insignia on the outside half of the right sleeve of the service coat and shirt, four inches above the end of the sleeve.

The Fifth Air Force was the major USAAF combat organization in the Pacific Region and was based in Australia after the Battle of the Philippines (1941-19420). Moving with the Allied ground forces, the USAAF Fifth Air Force established a series of airfields, some at existing facilities, but most were carved out of the jungle to provide tactical air support of the ground forces. The 5th Air Force is the oldest continuously-serving Numbered Air Force. It has provided 75 years of continuous air power to the Pacific since its establishment in 1941.

Meritorious Service Certificate

Meritorious Unit Commendation Ribbon

Meritorious Unit Commendation Emblem

The Meritorious Unit Commendation emblem worn to represent award of the Meritorious Unit Commendation is 1 7/16 inches wide and 9/16 inch in height. The emblem consists of a 1/16 inch wide Gold frame with laurel leaves which encloses a Scarlet 67111 ribbon. The previously authorized emblem was a Gold color embroidered laurel wreath, 1 5/8 inches in diameter on a 2 inches square of Olive Drab cloth.

Bronze Star
Awarded circa March 1944

The idea for the Bronze Star Medal was conceived in 1943 as a ground equivalent of the Air Medal. The idea rose through military bureaucracy until General George C. Marshall wrote the following memorandum to President Franklin D. Roosevelt, "The fact that ground troops lead lives of extreme discomfort and are often in personal combat with the enemy makes the maintenance of their morale of great importance, suffering the heaviest losses in the Army and enduring the greatest hardships.

President Roosevelt authorized the Bronze Star Medal by Executive Order 9419 dated February 4, 1944.

William H. Calhoon wrote to his father from New Guinea on March 13, 1944 that "My outfit has been awarded the Bronze Star for the campaign for New Guinea. He added, "I saw General MacArthur. I can't tell you where it was, but, anyway, I can now say I have seen him in person."

The Family of William (Bill) Harvey Calhoon

Grandparents

Joseph Bear (Civil War Veteran)   Mary E. (Shetron) Bear

Parents

John D. Calhoon, Sr.   Mary Bear Calhoon
  b. 1886; d. 1977   b. 1890; d. 1934

Aunt

Known as Bert, sister of John D. Calhoon, Sr.

Siblings

Minnie Calhoon, first born child who died in infancy

George Calhoon   Irene (Randolph) Calhoon
  b. 07/08/1910   b. 09/16/1913
  d. 05/18/2004   d. 05/13/1993

  Lived mainly in Wormleysburg

Clarence Calhoon   Gertrude "Doll" (Hipple) Calhoon
  b. 12/06/1911   b. 09/19/1914
  d. 2/12/1980   d. 05/16/1993

  Lived in Middletown & Royalton

  Child: Donna

John D. Calhoon, Jr.   Elizabeth (Scheib) Calhoon
  b. 09/12/1913   b. 01/01/1918
  d. 05/05/1993   d. 10/21/1997

  Lived on Derry St. in Harrisburg

  Child: Carol

Mary Calhoon Shellhamer
b. 02/04/1916
d. 01/15/2001

Frank Shellhamer
b. 04/08/1913
d. 01/15/1992

Lived mainly on Geyers' Church Rd., Londonderry Township
Child: Larry

Francis Calhoon

b. 1917
d. 1978

Catharine "Kitty" (College)
Calhoon
b. 1929
d. 2000

Lived on Geyers' Church Road, Londonderry Township

Helen Calhoon Bradley Attick
b. 1921
d. 2005

Robert Attick
b. 1915
d. 1991

Lived on a farm north of Rutherford
Children: Barbara Ann Bradley and a son, Barry W. Bradley, who died in infancy

William H. Calhoon

b. 09/12/1922
d. 12/19/2000

Geraldine "Jerry" (Heisey)
Calhoon
b. 12/24/1923
d. 12/23/2015

Edgar Calhoon
b. 04/25/1924
d. 09/30/2009

Virginia (Witters) Calhoon
b. 1933

Lived in Hummelstown, Geyer's Church Road, and Middletown
Children: Robin, Roger, Jeffrey

Madeline C. Calhoon, the last born child who died in infancy
b. 05/03/1926
d. 07/15/1926

Children

William H. Calhoon, Jr. (Diane Mundorf)
b. May 31, 1943

Children: Wendy Chicoria and Brent Calhoon

Dr. Janet E. Calhoon (widow of John Seavers)
b. June 15, 1948

June C. Mooney (John)
b. June 15, 1948

Ann C. Wagner (Robert L.)
b. April 5, 1958

Family
Memories

Memories of Dad

I recall my father as a strict disciplinarian, at least until I turned 18, had just finished high school, and was about to begin my summer job in the Hershey Chocolate factory where he also worked. I had the 7-3 shift and his advice to me was "If you think you can come in late and be up in time to work all day at the factory, you're welcome to try."

Dad also was very involved with me and my activities, including serving as our Boy Scout leader, even going to scout camp, using one of his two weeks of vacation to be a part of this. In my teens we went hunting together a few times, he encouraged me to go on my own a few times, and we also fished together occasionally. I also remember family day trips to various state parks so that the family could have some fun times together.

Dad seldom talked about right and wrong; instead, he showed by everything he did the way he wanted us to treat others and live our lives. I vividly remember that he and I frequently went to the homes of older people in town to pick their fruit trees for them (sometimes keeping some for our family, at their insistence). That was Dad, pitching in to help other people in town without any expectation of payment.

I remember one special time when my own family lived in Scranton that my parents, close to the age of 70, drove up to help us strip wallpaper, a very tedious job which took patience and endurance. That was such a help to us and the basis for later laughter.

William, Jr.

My Memories of Dad

I remember Mom saying Dad had trouble getting Bill to warm up to him when dad came home from the war. He won Bill over by pushing him in a stroller. When June and I arrived he pushed us in a stroller so much the wheels needed to be replaced. When I first opened my office years ago, more than one patient told me they remembered my dad pushing his twins in the stroller.

Mom worked evenings at Rhoads Pharmacy for years. Dad was the parent who went to PTA meetings, parent-teacher conferences, Band Parent meetings and others. He demonstrated his love and support for us by coming to band concerts in elementary school; listening to beginning instrumental students truly takes a parent's love. In high school, it was band competitions and attending football games to see the half time shows. He was a Middletown alumnus. I think he debated with himself every year which side of the field to sit on at that game, and as I remember he chose Lower Dauphin because it was the high school of his children.

He took us to Harrisburg to see the State Capital and the State Museum and we always made time to go to Mr. Peanut and get peanuts to feed the squirrels. I thought everyone's dad did these activities but I found out later that isn't the case.

At our house, it was Dad who got up in the middle of the night when one of us was sick. At some point, as an older child or perhaps when we were adults, that fact came into conversation. Dad laughed and said if Mom had gotten up to clean up after a sick kid (he always called us his kids, never his children) he would have had two messes to clean up.

I graduated from chiropractic college in Davenport, Iowa on December 17, 1971 and accepted a position in Monongahela, Pennsylvania. Dad and I drove most of the distance in an awful ice storm. The freezing rain was so heavy that the second car missed the first one exiting the highway because the driver couldn't see. This was before cell phones, and GPS. There were CB radios but we didn't have one.

Two years later I left Monongahela and came back to Hummelstown. This move was also in December and bad winter weather for the drive. I think it wasn't long after that second move dad told me if I moved again in the winter, he wanted to know about it after it was over. That's what he said but I knew if I needed him, he'd be there and never complain, just always ready to help.

Jan

Million Dollar Memories of Dad
Upon his 75th Birthday

—June Calhoon, 1997

An early memory I have of my Dad
Is rocking in a rocking chair that we had.
He wasn't just sitting there as some folks do,
He always had a kid in his lap, maybe two.

Afternoon walks down the railroad tracks,
We'd walk for awhile, and then we'd head back.
We even crossed the trestle without too much fear,
It was a long way down, but Dad was near!

Although he worked hard he was never too busy,
He never complained that his kids made him dizzy!
He planted a garden for our food to grow,
While I think one row of beans is too much to hoe!

He loves picking fruit, his favorite is cherries,
But we've also had treats from his picking wild berries.
When he went berry picking, we sent him alone;
Tales of snakes that Mom told kept us kids at home.

Patience is a virtue of which he has a lot,
But did he pass this onto his kids? I think not!
He helped us to walk, to ride our bikes,
Our time together we really liked!

When we were kids, he even cooked,
But as he's gotten older, he's dropped that book.
He does make coffee, without which life would be tough,
But you'll have to admit, making coffee isn't really rough.

I don't remember him raising his voice,
But loving discipline was clearly his choice.
I don't remember the method, but I clearly know the man,
And I'm glad his being our Dad was part of God's plan.

We got older and went out on our own,
But he still makes time for us, sometimes by phone.
He visits in our homes, works while he's there,
But don't ask him to sit still, not even on a dare!

Millions of dollars he never made;
But our million dollar memories won't ever fade.
Some were made when we were young, others as we grew,
But our Father's love we always knew!

                    I love you, Dad.

Bill Calhoon at Retirement

In school days, friends would call him Buck,
A school bus ride was unheard of luck.
He walked each day to school and back,
They didn't have a gym, but exercise didn't lack.

He came to Hershey in June of '41,
The box department is where he'd begun.
In the community building he did abide
Until a wife was by his side.

July of nineteen-forty-two
Was when he and Jerry said, "I do."
Married life was really great
But they sure didn't have time to celebrate.

World War II had begun
No more time for any fun.
December 8, '41 the U.S. entered in
And Bill was to be part of the team that would win.

November of nineteen-forty-two
Uncle Sam called him too.
New Guinea, Okinawa and the Philippines he saw,
It wasn't vacation, it was the law.

Proud he was that he could be
Part of the force that kept us free.
But, oh how happy was the day
The war was over and he came to stay.

But who was waiting for him? Not just a wife,
A little son had entered his life.
Bill Jr. — 29 months old
Before his Daddy's arms did hold.

Back to the factory he did go
It was a steady job you know.
It wasn't to the box department that he was sent
Instead to the cocoa department he went.

'46 was the year he changed his gear
And moved from cocoa to condensing,
To change no more was to be his store,
He's been there since reminiscing.

And then in nineteen-forty-eight
Something happened that was really great!
Twin daughters were added to his home.
Now he and his wife were never alone.

Ten years passed as a family of five
And they were happy to be alive.
Playing, working, learning together,
In all kinds of days and all kinds of weather.

In '58 the family did grow
Another girl God did bestow.
Raising four kids is no small feat
So now the family was complete.

What makes him great?
Why does he rate
As the world's number one dad
And the best ever mate?

I'll tell you why,
Or at least I'll try.
It's what he showed us by his example
That's given our lives a great preamble.

A love for God and country, too.
Honesty, integrity in all we do.
Working hard is but our fate
It doesn't matter if we're not great.

This man is patience personified,
Kindness his life exemplifies.
Time for his children is his life's rule
He's a marvelous dad, not someone's fool.

He gave his life as a young man
To the One before whom we all shall stand.
Jesus Christ is His Lord
And by this man He is adored.

Dad taught us how to work and play
He taught us how to live each day.
But more than for this life alone,
He pointed us to God's royal throne.

Tall, dark and handsome — maybe not,
But a whole lot more than that, he's got.
Laughter, sportsmanship and hospitality
Our Dad shows love to the "Nth" degree.

He may not be rich in money and land,
But he has done his best to stand
Against what's wrong and do what's right
To serve his God with all his might.

We're proud of him, we love him much,
What doesn't matter is money and such.
He's shown us life is more than a toy,
To do what's right is what brings joy.

He's Bill to you, he's Dad to me
And others call him Baldy, you see
It's not the name that makes one mount
But how you live is what really counts.

Hershey candy is the best,
It paid the bills and we were blessed
To have a Dad who had a job
That was secure, he never need rob.

It allowed him to be at home each night.
To play with his kids, to turn out the lights.
He didn't have to travel, he loved his home
And far from it, he did not roam.

June Calhoon
January 5, 1986

It All Began in Forty-Two, When Mom and Dad said,

"Yes, I do!"

When June wrote the following on the 50th Anniversary of the marriage of her father and mother, she wrote it as a tribute and a snapshot of her parents' lives together. She could not have known how fittingly this piece would parallel the story told in this book.

When Bill and Jerry got engaged
They wouldn't know world war soon would rage.
As for the wedding, no date yet set,
They just enjoyed romance, you can bet.

December 7, 1941 brought our country into war,
But no one could know what was in store.
Bill was serving in the Guard; there was no doubt
His time as a civilian was running out.

Their love was young, but it held true.
The thought of parting made them blue.
The decision was made to share their life
And go through the war as husband and wife.

July 18, 1942 was the day
Their married life got under way.
Bill to his country was on call,
So, on their honeymoon, Gettysburg they saw.

A month later the separation came;
Bill to Fort Riley, life was never the same.
Jerry, pregnant, at home she did wait
Wondering what life would bring to her mate.

New Guinea is where Bill spent his time
When his son was born and did just fine.
Jerry missed Bill much, writing many a letter,
But needed to see him to really feel better.

Jerry got her wish in nineteen forty-five
When Bill came home, very much alive.
She cried, although not from dread,
The tears were due to Bill's bald head.

With a full head of hair he once had been blessed,
But without it Jerry did not love him less.
To see it gone was a great surprise,
She couldn't hide the jolt even with lies.

She really was glad he was once again home,
Never again from her side would he roam.
His hair was gone, but not his heart.
From that time on they would never part.

Their dreams at last had now come true,
And their life together they did renew.
The war was over, but not their love;
They felt God's safety from high above.

Back to Hershey Chocolate Bill did go
Where a steady income he did know.
Making chocolate was part of the plan;
No wonder he remained such a very sweet man.

The twins were born in forty-eight;
This time Bill was home on the date.
He had waited 29 months to hold his son,
Daughters he held when their lives had begun.

Young Bill was five when the girls were born,
And never would he ever forget that morn.
Twin girls in the house brought lots of work,
But from this task Mom and Dad didn't shirk.

A family of five, they worked and played,
343 West Main is where they stayed.
Bill at the factory, Jerry at Rhoads,
The family sped through food and clothes.

Tired of toys of every assortment,
Nanny and Pap soon chose an apartment.
After that their house was sold.
"215 West Second" the young family then was told.

A baby girl joined the family in the two years there,
But as everyone knows, she did not get in Bill's hair.
Their stay in this house was really quite brief,
And in 1960 the family turned still another leaf.

This time to 26 East High they went,
From this house Bill, Jr., to college was sent.
In four years he was graduated from there,
Then on to Pensacola and into the air.

Cutting classes was against the rule
When Jan and June went to school.
Graduating, and then off to college,
Mom and Dad bought their own small cottage.

Into the country, out from the town,
Owning this place sent away all frowns.
Living in Stoverdale was quite unique
But driving that lane was no small feat.

Ann had to change schools, what a chore!
But she made it through with quite a score.
Good grades, and a scholarship, too,
Helped pay her way all college through.

You thought the family had then stopped growing?
Then you really can't be in the knowing.
Brother Bill soon gained a beautiful wife,
Diane brought much joy into his life.

Then grandchildren came, Wendy and Brent,
These were gifts that heaven had sent
Into the lives of Bill and Jerry,
As Brent and Wendy made them quite merry.

A man named Johnny became Jan's mate,
While John became June's at a later date.
Ann, still single, doesn't regret it,
Living alone she loves every minute.

Jan's a doctor, as everyone knows,
She does so much to lessen Mom and Dad's woes.
June lives in Florida with lots of sun,
It's there from the cold that she did run.

Ann has her own place in Sherman's Dale,
Mom and Dad's welcome there will never pale.
It, too, is away from the city,
Her joy at that could make one giddy.

Retirement, too, has entered the scene,
But sitting still is not so keen.
Working part time, traveling some,
Visiting family, they have lots of fun.

Fifty years as one another's mate,
We gather today to celebrate.
Our thanks to each of you, we say,
For helping us honor them today.

                               – June Calhoon

What It's Like to be a Twin

"What's it like to be a twin?" is a question often posed,
Why not ask, "What's it like to be a person?" why everyone really knows...
Every person is different and so their answer would be,
"What's it like to be a person? I can only answer for me."

A twin is like a person, no different don't you see,
Two may look alike, and yet be as different as can be!
Now being Jan's twin, is something unique
And from that perspective, I can speak.

We've had our ins and outs, our highs and our lows,
But of our friends close to us, everyone knows
When down on our luck, even down and out,
We'll stick together without any doubt.

Our school years were bumpy, we argued a lot,
And even on cold days, our tempers got hot.
If she liked something, you could bet your money,
For sure I wouldn't like it, it was kind of funny.

After high school we drifted apart,
She went to college, I entered the job mart.
She went to Arkansas, I hung around home,
But it wasn't long before we both did roam.

She went to Iowa to become a doctor,
I went to college to learn how to proctor.
A chiropractor she came to be
And teaching kids grew dear to me.

After college graduation, she returned to her homeland,
I went to Nassau to teach, and to play in the sand.
Remember I said the same things we like — NOT!
She likes the weather cold, and I like it hot!

In Pennsylvania she came to stay
While in warmer climates I live each day.
No longer in Nassau, I'm still close to the bay,
But now my home is in the U.S.A.

Through the years and through some tears,
We've each made many friends, they're all dears.
Friends may come and friends may go,
But life is twins for us, we always know.

The years and life's experiences have mellowed both of us,
So that when we have our differences, we don't make any fuss.
There was a time when we both were much afraid
If the other knew our weakness, she'd really have it made.

But God is good and patience He has got,
And He has worked in both of us and taught us a whole lot.
So now instead of cheering when the other one is down,
We do our best to help her so she doesn't keep a frown.

Jan gave me courage, she believed in me,
She rescued me when I couldn't get free
With her help I made it through.
And the hard times, well, they weren't just a few!

On holidays and special occasions our clan gathers at her home,
With a place to rest and a place to eat, there's no need to roam.
Then beds are made, dishes done, and laundry before we go,
Jan really doesn't like domestic, in case you didn't know.

Remember the question I posed at the start?
"What's it like to be a twin, to really hold the part?"
Remember each pair is different, and may give a different reply,
But here is more about us, not one word is any lie.

We don't have, and we never did, any extra special perception,
Our knowledge of the other in no way reaches perfection.
We don't know when the other is truly feeling sick,
Or what she thinks or when she blinks or what really makes her tick.

We have heard the stories of twins who can do such,
But as for me personally, they don't have credence much.
In second grade we once changed seats in school,
And I must say that teach, well, she wasn't any fool!

Nor was a sense of humor something she did possess,
I'll never forget that academic experience never the less.
But in later years being twins gave both of us a smile,
Although we were separated by mile after mile after mile.

In this country's airports we have both been mistaken,
Not recognizing close friends has sometimes left them shaken.
But then they'd ask, "Don't you remember me?"
Our answer came quickly, "You must know my twin, not me."

I hope these words have given to each one some insight,
To know what it's like to be a twin, perhaps I've shed some light.
Twins are different and alike at the same time.
There's no way to explain it, no reason nor any rhyme.

Thank you, Jan, for all you've done and all you mean to me,
I'm glad you are my sister and that twins we'll always be.
So with these words, I'll close my part,
I love you, Jan, with all of my heart.

My Dad

My father was a man of his word and his faith. I always knew that he loved his children and his wife. I don't remember ever wondering why he loved his children, but as I reached high school and college age, I often wondered why he loved my mother so much. It wasn't until I was much older that I realized Dad was teaching me the meaning of unconditional love, not from some textbook, but by simply living it out in front of me every day.

I remember Dad often acting as family peacemaker, not so often between my siblings and me, because of the age difference (ten years with my sisters and fifteen with my brother) involved, but between Mom and me. There was no doubt I got my temper from Mom. We were so much alike that conflicts were unavoidable. I do know that he would often tell me that she loved me but wasn't very comfortable showing love or talking about it. Dad would also say that if things were going to get better, I would have to be the one to mend the rift. I always believed that he loved both of us but I learned to realize that he also loved a quiet house.

What I learned most to appreciate was that Dad never told me there was anything I couldn't do because I was a girl. There were things I couldn't do because we couldn't afford them, but my gender was never a reason for not doing something.

When I wanted to play tackle football with the boys on the block, that was fine with him until I got glasses, which he couldn't afford to replace if they got broken. When I wanted to go fishing and hunting with him, he took me. When I became interested in science and biology, there were no negative comments about my digging in the ground or dissecting dead animals to learn more about them.

When plans for my future involved living alone and working to support myself, Dad supported me. He never even implied that I should get married, stay at home and raise children. I don't remember ever being aware of any gender bias from my teachers or professors, either.

However, once I started working, almost all of my managers were white males Dad's age or a little younger. I had several of them actually tell me I should not be working outside the home at all because I might be taking a job away from a man. If I had to work to support myself, then it should be something feminine, like answering telephones, where I could wear a dress while I was waiting for some man to come along and marry me.

It was actually a culture shock, but because I had many years with Dad of being told I could do anything I wanted, I relied on that to survive. I'm not sure I ever told my Dad how grateful I was for this aspect of how he raised me, but he knew me so well I am sure he understood.

—Ann Calhoon Wagner

Endnotes

World War II: 1941–June 1943 Endnotes

1   There is a paver bearing Joseph Bear's name at the Civil War Museum in Harrisburg, PA, donated by Roger Calhoon.

2   The highest number of enlistees in any single year in any war.

3   Evans, Harold. (1998). The American Century. NY: Alfred A. Knopf. p. 309.

4   Ibid., p. 27.

5   The 1942 Echo, Curwensville, Pennsylvania

6   The 1942 Tatler, p. 5.

7   Center of Excellence, Military Police Battalion

8   Duration was a new term used to mean for however long it took to win the War. Wakefield, Dan. (1982). Under the Apple Tree. NY: Delacorte Press, p. 48.

9   Unconfirmed.

10 Built mainly by the Army Corps of Engineers constructing this highway had been discussed for years; the war provided the impetus needed to finish it. Although the highway was completed on October 28, 1942 and its completion was celebrated at Soldier's Summit on November 21, the "highway" was not usable by general vehicles until 1943.

11 This is another name for ceremoniously lowering the flag and folding it properly.

12 With this we note that Bill had three brothers who also served in WWII, Francis, Clarence, and Edgar.

13 The Air Corps was the immediate predecessor of the United States Army Air Force (USAAF), established in June 1941. Although discontinued as an administrative echelon during WWII, the Air Corps (AC) remained as one of the combat arms of the Army until 1947, when it was legally abolished by legislation establishing the Department of the Air Force.

14 The USO was an organization which oversaw and provided recreation and aid services for the men and women of the United States Armed Forces. The types of USO services offered were clubs, lounges and traveler's aid service, overseas service camp shows to entertain the military troops and much more.

15 Slang for baby.

16   This is in reference to Hillsdale Road, an area outside of Middletown; Hillsdale and Geyer's Church Road form the intersection at which Geyer's Church is located.

17   https://www.nps.gov/nR/travel/wwIIbayarea/embarkation.htm

18   http://ww2troopships.com/crossings/1944b.htm

WW II: July 1943–December 1943 Endnotes

1 Laffin, John (1986). Brassey's Battles: 3,500 Years of Conflict, Campaigns and Wars from A-Z. London: Brassey's Defence Publishers, p. 303. ISBN 0080311857.

2 http://postalmuseum.si.edu/victorymail/letter/

3 The author, in first grade at the time, remembers asking the neighbors, who had a relative serving in the Army, if she could help them write letters to their nephew, Jim Wilt, understanding only that this is what people should be doing.

4 This included this author who wanted to be part of the war effort beyond singing at Bond Rallies and who for years later wondered how the flimsy paper letters were not torn.

5 From all indications, the "spending money" of military men in the Philippines would be that of Australia, which is based on the British system.

6 Just this simple comment reaffirms how important getting mail was to the men.

7 This confirms what an early reviewer of this book said about how important it was to find someone "overseas" that was from one's own hometown.

8 This could possibly mean that children were being fathered (unplanned) by some of the soldiers.

9 There are two possible interpretation here of "becoming more white." The first is the number of babies fathered by the military and the second that the natives were being influenced culturally

10 Winnie Shultz married John Rider during this time; their sons are Kevin and Keith Rider.

11 The C-Ration, or Type C Ration, was an individual canned, pre-cooked, and prepared wet ration. It was intended to be issued to U.S. military land forces when fresh food (A-Ration) or packaged unprepared food (B-Ration) prepared in mess halls or field kitchens was not possible or not available.

¹² Aunt Bert was possibly married to one of Pap's brothers, thereby being Bert Calhoon.

¹³ Again, the importance of a contact from "home."

¹⁴ Referring to the Bismarck Archipelago, a group of islands off the northeastern coast of New Guinea in the western Pacific Ocean.

¹⁵ A small island in the Netherlands East Indies (NEI), which the Allies used as a base to support the liberation of the Philippines.

Interlude Endnotes

1   In his book "Fu-Go: The Curious History of Japan's Balloon Bomb Attack on America," author Ross Coen called the weapon "the world's first intercontinental ballistic missile," and the silent delivery of death from pilotless balloons has been referred to as World War II's version of drone warfare.

2   While there were 2,000 small shops in New York City (Stern, Rudi (1988). *The New Let There Be Neon*. H. N. Abrams. pp. 16–33) using neon signs by 1940, neon signs were still not plentiful in small towns. (The author clearly remembers this government prohibition order and that she had asked her parents what neon meant.)

World War II: 1944 Endnotes

1   *Our American Century*, "Decade of Triumph – The 40s", p. 64.

2   It perhaps should be mentioned that while most colleges were losing enrollment of males (including those who played football), the Military Academies were not. Rather, they were at full enrollment.

3   The Lend-Lease Act, passed in 1941, gave President Roosevelt the power to sell to sell, transfer, exchange, lease, or lend equipment to any country to help it defend itself against the Axis powers.

4   Forever after identified as the voice of "God Bless America."

5   Detached Service means military service away from one's assigned organization, unit, etc. This is also an indicator to the reader that Bill's unit was temporarily being pulled out for a special assignment.

6   Abbreviation likely for the area Bill was at the time of writing this letter.

7   Nip is an ethnic slur against people of Japanese descent and origin, similar to the ethnic slur Jap, widely used during this time. The word *Nip* is an abbreviation from *Nippon*, the Japanese name for Japan.

8   Bill is likely responding to a question from his father about the war.

9   APO 322 is Base F, Finschhafen, New Guinea.

10 Pud was fighting in the European Theatre.

11 Pud was part of the North African Invasion.

12 According to Bill's family, their father thought very highly of MacArthur and after the war Bill had told his children that if President Truman had allowed the General to do what he wanted to do (militarily), there would not have been a Korean War.

13 This is so telling of the times. There was an extra *assurance* among those of marrying age to get married (especially if the men were of draft age) as an unvoiced statement and confidence that there would be a future.

14 A confirmation that their letters were reviewed.

15 There were numerous military camps built in the Central Louisiana area, a significant part of the massive U.S. military build-up specifically to support the war effort, with Alexandria camp a major one.

16 This likely is in reference to their company being moved again, but still not being on a ship homeward bound. It is also possible that this is referring to comrades who traveled by boat on leave or furlough, while Bill's turn hadn't yet come up.

17 Confirmation that, yes, they had been moved.

18 APO 321 is Mindoro, Philippines.

19 Likely in reference to their being on special mission and not at their regular base.

20 Likely a hernia.

21 Another example that many citizens in home towns who knew those in service sent them letters.

22 This is in reference to taking medicine (preventive or otherwise) for diseases that might be encountered in the jungle.

23 These comments, as well as others Bill has made in his letters, are an indication as to why the military went to great lengths to keep the mail moving through such faster processes as V-Mail.

24 The number written in Bill's letter wasn't clear, so this may be in error.

25 APO 920 is Base H, Biak, Dutch New Guinea.

26 The World Series teams were in the same city. Fans from either team could take public transportation to either field for five cents.

27 Another hint or indication that Bill was a part of the road-building projects, as family have indicated.

28 Here referring to Pud's being part of the Normandy Invasion.

29 Interesting at the cavalier reference to a foxhole as what Bill says is certainly an indicator of being on the front line.

30 The term "fox hole" originated in WWII to identify one of the "defensive fighting positions."

31 Larry, Barbara Ann, and Billy.

32 Referring to Pud's being part of the Normandy Invasion.

33 Jessie Pifer estate papers.

34 APO 72 is Tacloban, Leyte, Philippines.

35 USC won 25-0.

World War II: 1945 Endnotes

1 Don Miller was not alone in suffering what today would be called a post-traumatic stress disorder. Many brave soldiers were the quiet victims in wars and even two of the Calhoon servicemen were thought (in retrospect) to have experienced this syndrome after valorous service in the fields, the sky, and the oceans.

2 A break from service, as he had been a part of many major invasions and was due for leave.

3 The use of the term "APO" was first established in San Francisco, March 3, 1944. APO was first used as the mailing code for Base K, Tacloban, Leyte, Philippine Islands, beginning October 20, 1944, the same date as the US Forces under the command of General MacArthur landed at Leyte to begin the liberation of The Philippines. APO 72 was discontinued May 31, 1946.

4 There is, of course, no way to know when Clam had last written to Bill, because he likely would not have dared mention the battle or the typhoon. It is even possible that Clam had written prior to this naval battle and it would be harmless simply to tell his brother that he might be coming out his way.

5 This is just one example of what was stated somewhat generally and casually. Bill likely knew what some of the tactical plans were since his outfit had helped build the airfields.

6 Bill's assessment of this is borne out by the record. The objective of the Japanese was to lessen the morale of the lonely American soldiers, but nearly all of them saw through this ruse.

7 Mindoro, The Philippines.

8 This is as much as could be stated and is part of the reason that many families had maps mounted in their homes to track any clue they might gain from the letters as to where their loved one was.

9 Command Performance (1942-49) was a radio show broadcast by the military. Servicemen were encouraged to write to the show to request their favorite stars and make suggestions. The stars performed free of charge and free performances by celebrities for the military became a tradition.

10 In retrospect we can see these comments as clues as to what was going to happen.

11 This is a good indicator that the troops have some idea of the overall strategy and of the strength of the U.S. Forces.

12 Knowing how Bill understates any difficulty, we can be sure this was a rough stretch.

13 This is an example of the military's intention to rotate the troops so at least they had some restoration time (unless, of course, everyone was needed in an offensive drive or a defensive position).

14 It is likely that Bill was making a joke here. 4-F was the classification for those unfit for service.

15 Skip is John, Jr., the third son in the family.

16 Slim Alleman was a neighbor to the Calhoons.

17 An area from which to rest from battle; a support area, not a front line.

18 710 was the APO for the 5th Air Force and was not always the same physical location, but moved with the unit.

19 There are two possible explanations here. One is that "going G.I." meant they would again have to be in uniform most of the time. Another explanation could be that soldiers and airmen sardonically referred to themselves as "G.I." meaning "General Issue" items, as disposable as helmets, boots, tents, canteens, rifles, jeeps, trucks, tanks, and combat aircraft. They viewed themselves as being "General Issue" items of "Uncle Sam" while they were in military service. Those who took that view saw the division of their unit almost as a demotion, no longer "special forces" that they had been doing with the 5th Air Force.

20 Garrison refers to the troops stationed in a place, particularly a town, to defend it. Not a high powered position.

21 Landing ship, tank.

22 "White" here meaning they have no tan.

23   It is not that Bill is forgetful. Eggy has been moving from camp to camp, place to place, just as Bill has, so it would be difficult for Bill to be kept informed by any mail from Eggy.

24   "Sort of busy" was putting it mildly. Major engagements surrounded Bill. Allied Forces were positioned for a final assault on Japan—perhaps the last of them, and his father evidently is concerned about the lack of having someone to help him at home. How gentle and respectful Bill is, downplaying the severity of the situation on Luzon by the simple words, I am "sort of busy."

25   Likely Jerry was referring to an Easter service. Again a reminder of just how long it took for some letters to travel from the States to the Pacific.

26   Again, the respect Bill shows to his father who would like a "souvenir" from the war, an understandable request, but so telling that those at home had no possible understanding that the troops were in the middle of a major engagement. Likely victory in Europe had many at home feeling like the war was over.

27   It is hard to imagine being away from home already for almost three years and never having seen one's son, now two years old.

28   It is almost impossible to comprehend the number of servicemen who had not seen their families for years.

29   Bill's unit is part of the 5th Air Force.

30   See endnote xix.

31   See endnote xx.

32   That would be three years of service.

33   Morison, Samuel E. (1965). *History of the American People,* p.1043. NY: Oxford University Press.

34   Situation Normal, All Fouled Up.

35   This would be May or June 1946.

36   Note the caution here.

37   Four days after his cautious statement in his previous letter, Bill makes this declaration, indicating they had been given the green light on this information.

38   Referring to "short subjects" as films shorter in length and focused on a single, specific subject.

39   Referring to the military film crews.

40   Information found in the personal log book of Mr. LeRoy G. Carter in *Troopships of World War II* by Roland W. Charles, published by The Army Transportation Association, Washington, D.C., 1947.

41   A term of "good-natured kidding" respect for an officer.

Credits:

Roger and Yvonne Calhoon, who contributed family information.

Wade S. Alexander, who reviewed the book pre-publication.

Notes:

CPSIA information can be obtained
at www.ICGtesting.com
Printed in the USA
BVOW08*1935130117

473408BV00002B/2/P